First World War
and Army of Occupation
War Diary
France, Belgium and Germany

50 DIVISION
Divisional Troops
Divisional Ammunition Column
5 August 1914 - 30 June 1919

WO95/2820/3

The Naval & Military Press Ltd
www.nmarchive.com
Published in association with The National Archives

Published by

The Naval & Military Press Ltd

Unit 10 Ridgewood Industrial Park,

Uckfield, East Sussex,

TN22 5QE England

Tel: +44 (0) 1825 749494

www.naval-military-press.com

www.nmarchive.com

This diary has been reprinted in facsimile from the original. Any imperfections are inevitably reproduced and the quality may fall short of modern type and cartographic standards.

© **Crown Copyright**
Images reproduced by permission of The National Archives, London, England, 2015.

Contents

Document type	Place/Title	Date From	Date To
Heading	WO95/2820 50 Div Ammunition Column Aug 14-May 19		
Heading	50th Division 50th Divl Ammn Column 1914 Aug May 1919		
Heading	50th Division 3rd Nortn Bde R.F.A. Ammn Coln Vol I		
War Diary	Durham	05/08/1914	15/08/1914
War Diary	Nawcastle	21/08/1914	21/08/1914
War Diary	Ravensworth	05/11/1914	05/11/1914
War Diary	How Fell	09/11/1914	09/11/1914
War Diary	Sunderland Area	29/01/1915	29/01/1915
War Diary	How Fell	17/04/1915	17/04/1915
War Diary	Southampton	18/04/1915	18/04/1915
War Diary	Havre	19/04/1915	20/04/1915
War Diary	Hazebrouck	21/04/1915	21/04/1915
War Diary	Rouqe Goix	22/04/1915	23/04/1915
War Diary	Mout De Cals	24/04/1915	24/04/1915
War Diary	Rouqe Goix	25/04/1915	25/04/1915
War Diary	Rattakot	26/04/1915	26/04/1915
War Diary	Vlamertinghe	27/04/1915	27/04/1915
War Diary	Watou	05/05/1915	05/05/1915
War Diary	Rattekot	26/04/1915	26/04/1915
War Diary	St Laurent	27/04/1915	27/04/1915
War Diary	He Sample	06/05/1915	06/05/1915
War Diary	Winnezeele	10/05/1915	10/05/1915
War Diary	Watou	13/05/1915	13/05/1915
War Diary	G 3 C	14/05/1915	14/05/1915
War Diary	Watou	18/05/1915	18/05/1915
War Diary	G 3 C	18/05/1915	18/05/1915
War Diary	Watou	19/05/1915	19/05/1915
War Diary	Sheet B. 36 B. 17 D.2.3	23/07/1915	24/07/1915
War Diary	B.21 A.7.2	25/07/1915	02/08/1915
Heading	50th Division 50th Divl Ammn Coln Vol I		
War Diary	Lealran Harbone Co. Durham	20/11/1914	06/04/1915
War Diary	Levenrtte An Ygne	10/04/1915	10/04/1915
War Diary	Park Royal	15/04/1915	31/07/1915
Heading	50th Division 2nd Northumbrian Bde RFA Ammn Coln Vol 1 18.4.-31.5.15		
Heading	War Diary of O.C. 2nd Northumbrian Am Col. From. 18.4.15 Vol I To 31.5.15.		
War Diary	Huvaslte	18/04/1915	18/04/1915
War Diary	Southampton	19/04/1915	19/04/1915
War Diary	Haure	20/04/1915	20/04/1915
War Diary	Hezeburuel	21/04/1915	21/04/1915
War Diary	Strazeele	22/04/1915	22/04/1915
War Diary	Eslqyale	23/04/1915	24/04/1915
War Diary	Watou	25/04/1915	26/04/1915
War Diary	W. Watou	27/04/1915	27/04/1915
War Diary	Winnezeele	27/04/1915	04/05/1915
War Diary	Mudnyln	04/05/1915	07/05/1915
War Diary	Winnezeele	08/05/1915	10/05/1915

War Diary	C St Grenter Buizer	10/05/1915	13/05/1915
War Diary	Ct Pt. G. 4. on Poperinghe Vlamertinghe Road	13/05/1915	13/05/1915
War Diary	Poperinghe Vlamertinghe Road	14/05/1915	18/05/1915
War Diary	Poperinghe Road	18/05/1915	19/05/1915
War Diary	Poperinghe Rd. G.4. C Map 23 Belgium N.W.	20/05/1915	21/05/1915
War Diary	Poperinghe Vlamertinghe Road	22/05/1915	27/05/1915
War Diary	St Jeanter Biezen	27/06/1915	30/06/1915
War Diary	Abeele	30/06/1915	30/06/1915
Heading	50th Division 2nd Northumbrian Bde Ammn Coln Vol II 1-30.6.15		
Heading	2nd Northumbrian Bde Amm Column War Diary 1/30. June 1915 Capt. H.W. Smales R.F.A. Vol II		
War Diary	Abeele	01/06/1915	04/06/1915
War Diary	Boeschepe	05/06/1915	20/06/1915
War Diary	Me Vodaigne	21/06/1915	30/06/1915
Heading	50th Division 1/2nd Northbn Bde RFA Ammn Coln Vol III 1-31-7-15		
Heading	War Diary of Capt H.W. Smales RFA 2 N'bn Am Col. July & 31 July Vol III		
War Diary	Mont Vidaigne	01/07/1915	16/07/1915
War Diary	Pont De Nieppe	17/07/1915	31/07/1915
Heading	50th Division 1/3rd 1/3rd North'bn Bde Ammn Coln RFA. Vol II From 1-31.8.15		
Heading	50th Division War Diary Of Lieut Colonel F.W. Staff 50th Divisional Ammunition Column From 1st August 1915 To 31st August 1915 Volume II		
War Diary	Nieppe	01/08/1915	30/08/1915
Heading	50th Division 2nd North Bde RFA Ammn Col Vol V August 1915		
War Diary	Pont De Nieppe	01/08/1915	19/09/1915
War Diary	Pont Nieppe	20/08/1915	20/08/1915
War Diary	Nieppe	21/08/1915	31/08/1915
Heading	50th Division 3rd North'bn Bde RFA Ammn Coln Vol III Sept 15		
War Diary	Nieppe	01/09/1915	30/09/1915
Heading	50th Division 2nd North'bn Bde R.F.A. Ammn Coln Vol VI Sept 15		
War Diary	Nieppe	01/09/1915	30/09/1915
Heading	War Diary Vol VII 1/9/15 To 30/9/15 2 Nbn Am. Col		
Heading	50th Division 50th Div Ammun Col Sep Oct 15 Vol III		
Heading	War Diary Of Lieut Colonel F.W. Cluff 50th Divisional Ammunition Column From 1st Septr 1915 To 31st Octr 1915 Volume I		
War Diary	Nieppe	03/09/1915	25/10/1915
Heading	50th Division 2nd North'bn Bde RFA Ammn Coln Vol VII Oct 15		
War Diary	Nieppe	01/10/1915	24/10/1915
War Diary	Caestre.	24/10/1915	31/10/1915
Heading	50th Div Ammn Col Nov Vol IV		
War Diary		01/11/1915	30/11/1915
Heading	50th Division 1/2nd Northumbrian Ammn Col Nov. Vol VIII		
War Diary	Yds Farm. 3000. S.W Of Caestre Map Ref. W.2.b. 9x7 Ref Sheet 27 1/40	01/11/1915	06/11/1915
War Diary	Farm S.W. of Caestre Map Ref Sheet 27 1/40,000 W.2.b 9.7	07/11/1915	08/11/1915

War Diary	Farm Borre E.1.b. B.7 Ref Map Sheet 36a.	09/11/1915	13/11/1915
War Diary	Borre	14/11/1915	19/11/1915
War Diary	Farm At Point E.1.6. 6.7 Sheet 36a	20/11/1915	25/11/1915
War Diary	Borre Farm at Point E. 1.b. 6x7 Sheet 36.a.	26/11/1915	30/11/1915
War Diary	Summary Rest Camp Ammunition Issued during the month		
Heading	War Diary 2 N Bn Am. Col. Vol IX From 1.11.15 To 30.11.15		
Heading	50th D. 2/Northn Ammn Col Dec Vol IX		
War Diary	Borre	01/12/1915	19/12/1915
War Diary	Borre Reninghelst	19/12/1915	19/12/1915
War Diary	Reninghelst G.22.d.1x4 Sheet 28	20/12/1915	24/12/1915
War Diary	Reninghelst Farm G.22.d.1x4	25/12/1915	31/12/1915
Heading	War Diary Of Lieut Colonel F.W. Cluff 50th Divisional Ammunition Column From 1/12/15 To 31/12/15 Volume V		
War Diary	Borre	01/12/1915	31/12/1915
Heading	50th 1/2 N'brian Ammn Col. Jan Vol X		
War Diary	Reninghelst Farm. G.22.d. 1x4	01/01/1916	31/01/1916
Heading	War Diary Of Lieut Col F.W. Cluff 50th Divisional Ammunition Column From 1/1/16 To 29/2/16 Volume VII		
War Diary	2 1/2 Lines J.W Of Poperinghe	01/01/1916	29/02/1916
Heading	50 2 Northbrian Am Col Feb Vol XI		
War Diary	Reninghelst. Farm G.22.d. 1x4	01/02/1916	12/02/1916
War Diary	Reninghelst. Farm G.22.d. 1x4 Sheet 28	13/02/1916	14/02/1916
War Diary	Reninghelst Farm G.22. D 1x4	15/02/1916	17/02/1916
War Diary	Reninghelst Farm G. 22.d. 1.4 Sheet 28	18/02/1916	23/02/1916
War Diary	Reninghelst Farm G 22.d. 1x4.	24/02/1916	29/02/1916
Heading	War Diary of 2 Nbn Am Col Vol XII		
Heading	1/2 Nbrn Bde RFA Am Col Vol II		
War Diary	Reninghelst Farm G.22.d 1x4 Sheet 28	01/03/1916	02/03/1916
War Diary	Reninghelst. G.22.d 1x4	03/03/1916	28/03/1916
War Diary	Reninghelst G 22. D 1x4 Sheet 28	29/03/1916	31/03/1916
Heading	War Diary 2 N Bn Am Col From 1.3.16 To 31.3.16 Vol XII		
Heading	War Diary Of Lieut Colonel F.W. Cluff. From 1.3.16 To 3.4.16. Volume X		
War Diary	Poperinghe	01/03/1916	25/03/1916
War Diary	Godewaersvelde	04/04/1916	04/04/1916
War Diary	Berthen	07/04/1916	30/04/1916
War Diary	Reninghelst G. 22.d 1.4	01/04/1916	04/04/1916
War Diary	Farm P.24. A.6.4. Sheet. 27	05/04/1916	06/04/1916
War Diary	Farm M. 21.c.1.8 Sheet 28 S.W.	07/04/1916	12/04/1916
War Diary	Mt Vidaigne M.21.c 1.8	13/04/1916	18/04/1916
War Diary	M.21. C.1.8 28. S.W.	19/04/1916	30/04/1916
Heading	War Diary of Lieut-Colonel Cluff. From 1.5.16 To 31.5.16. Volume X. Divisional Ammunition Column. 50th Division.		
War Diary	Godewaersvelde	01/05/1916	31/05/1916
Heading	War Diary of Lieut. Colonel Cluff From. 1.6.16 To 30.6.16. Volume X D.A.C. 50th Division.		
War Diary	Mt Noir	01/06/1916	30/06/1916
War Diary		29/06/1916	29/06/1916

Heading	War Diary Of Lieut. Colonel F.W. Cluff 50th Divisional Ammunition Column From 1st July To 31st July 1916 Volume 16		
War Diary	Mont Noir	01/07/1916	04/07/1916
War Diary	Westoutre	05/07/1916	28/07/1916
War Diary	Westoutre	01/07/1916	31/07/1916
Heading	War Diary Of Lieut Colonel F.W. Cluff. 50th Divisional Ammunition Column. From 1.8.16 To 31.8.16 Volume 17		
War Diary	Westoutre	01/08/1916	09/08/1916
War Diary	Godewaersvelde	09/08/1916	13/08/1916
War Diary	Boisbergues	12/08/1916	14/08/1916
War Diary	Bourdon	14/08/1916	15/08/1916
War Diary	Frechencourt	15/08/1916	17/08/1916
War Diary	Albert	18/08/1916	28/08/1916
Operation(al) Order(s)	Operation Order No. 1	07/08/1916	07/08/1916
Operation(al) Order(s)	Operation Order No 2	14/08/1916	14/08/1916
Operation(al) Order(s)	Operation Order No. 3	15/08/1916	15/08/1916
Miscellaneous			
Operation(al) Order(s)	Operation Order No. 4		
Heading	50th Divisional Artillery 50th. Divisional Ammunition Column September 1916.		
Heading	War Diary Of Lieut-Colonel Cluff. Commanding D.A.C. 50 Division. From September 1st To September 30th Volume		
War Diary	Albert	01/09/1916	08/09/1916
War Diary	Becourt Wood	08/09/1916	19/09/1916
War Diary	Fricourt	20/09/1916	30/09/1916
Operation(al) Order(s)	Operation Order No. 6	19/09/1916	19/09/1916
Operation(al) Order(s)	Operation Order No 5	09/09/1916	09/09/1916
Heading	War Diary Of Lieut-Colonel Cluff. Commanding D.A.C. 50. Division. From October 1-To October 31 1916 Volume 18		
War Diary	Fricourt 62.d.f3.6.	01/10/1916	31/10/1916
War Diary	Fricourt	01/11/1916	14/11/1916
War Diary	Beaucourt	15/11/1916	28/11/1916
Operation(al) Order(s)	Operation Order No 9		
War Diary	Becourt	01/12/1916	05/12/1916
War Diary	Fricourt	05/12/1916	31/12/1916
War Diary	Fricourt	01/01/1917	31/01/1917
War Diary	Mirvaux	29/01/1917	31/01/1917
Operation(al) Order(s)	Operation Order No. 10 50th Divisional Ammun Column.	28/01/1917	28/01/1917
War Diary	Mirvaux	01/02/1917	05/02/1917
War Diary	Vaire	06/02/1917	06/02/1917
Operation(al) Order(s)	50th Divisional Ammunition Column Operation Order No. 12	11/02/1917	11/02/1917
Operation(al) Order(s)	50th Divisional Ammunition Column Operation Order No 11	04/02/1917	04/02/1917
War Diary	Vaire	06/02/1917	28/02/1917
War Diary	Proyart	01/03/1917	26/03/1917
War Diary	Havernas	28/03/1917	28/03/1917
War Diary	Boisbergues	29/03/1917	29/03/1917
War Diary	Humbercourt	30/03/1917	30/03/1917
War Diary	Monchiet	31/03/1917	31/03/1917

Operation(al) Order(s)	Operation Order No 13 by Lieut Col F.W. Cluff., R.F.A. (T) Commanding 50th Divisional Ammunition Column.	20/03/1917	20/03/1917
Operation(al) Order(s)	Operation Order No. 14 by Lieut Col F.W. Cluff. R.F.A. (T) Commanding 50th Divisional Ammunition Column.	21/03/1917	21/03/1917
Operation(al) Order(s)	Operation Order No 15 by Lieut Colonel F.W. Cluff R.F.A. (T) Commanding 50th Divisional Ammunition Column.	27/03/1917	27/03/1917
Operation(al) Order(s)	Operation Order No 16 By Lieut Col F.W. Cluff. R.F.A. (T) Commanding 50th Divisional Ammunition Column.	29/03/1917	29/03/1917
Operation(al) Order(s)	Operation Order No 17 By Lieut Col F.W. Cluff. R.F.A. (T) Commanding 50th Divisional Ammunition Column.	30/03/1917	30/03/1917
Operation(al) Order(s)	Addendum to Operation Order No 17 by Lieut Colonel F.W. Cluff R.F.A. (T) Commanding 50th Divisional Ammunition Column.		
War Diary	Monchiet	01/04/1917	29/04/1917
Operation(al) Order(s)	Addendum To Operation Order No. 20 By Lieut Col M.C. Drury. R.A., Commanding 50th Divisional Ammunition Column.	15/05/1917	15/05/1917
Operation(al) Order(s)	Operation Order No. 20 By Lieut Col M.C. Drury., R.A. Commanding 50th Divisional Ammunition Column.	16/05/1917	16/05/1917
Operation(al) Order(s)	Operation Order No. 18 By Lieut Col F.W. Cluff., R.F.A. (T) Commanding 50th Divisional Ammunition Column.	17/04/1917	17/04/1917
Miscellaneous	Amendment To Operation Order No 18 By Lieut Col F.W. Cluff. R.F.A. (T)., Cmdg 50th D.A.C	17/04/1917	17/04/1917
Operation(al) Order(s)	Operation Order No. 19 By Lieut Col F.W. Cluff., R.F.A. (T). Commanding 50th Divisional Ammunition Column.	28/04/1917	28/04/1917
War Diary	Monchiet	01/04/1917	29/05/1917
War Diary	Beaurains	01/06/1917	30/06/1917
Operation(al) Order(s)	Operation Order No 21 By Lieut Col R.C. Drury., R.A. Commanding 50th Divisional Ammunition Column.	16/06/1917	16/06/1917
Miscellaneous	Amendments To Operation Order No 21 By Lieut Col R.C. Drury., Commanding 50th Divisional Ammunition Column.	16/06/1917	16/06/1917
War Diary	Beaurains	01/07/1917	31/08/1917
Heading	War Diary Of 50th Divisional Ammunition Column. From 1st September, 1917 To 30th September, 1917. Volume No 30.		
War Diary	Beaurains	01/09/1917	25/09/1917
War Diary	Ficheux	20/09/1917	20/09/1917
Operation(al) Order(s)	Operation Orders No 22 by Lieut Colonel R.C. Drury., R.A. Commanding 50th Divisional Ammunition Column.	04/09/1917	04/09/1917
Operation(al) Order(s)	Operation Order No 23 by Lieut Colonel R.C. Drury., R.A. Commanding 50th Divisional Ammunition Column.	18/09/1917	18/09/1917
Operation(al) Order(s)	Operation Order No 24 by Lieut Colonel R.C. Drury., R.A., Commanding 50th Divisional Ammunition Column.	19/09/1917	19/09/1917
War Diary	Ficheux	01/10/1917	22/10/1917

War Diary	Elverdinghe	24/10/1917	29/10/1917
Heading	War Diary Of 50th Divisional Ammunition Column. From 1.11.17, To 30.11.17 Volume No XXXII.		
War Diary	Elverdinghe	01/11/1917	27/11/1917
Operation(al) Order(s)	Operation No. 28 (Part II) Relief Table.		
War Diary	Vlamertinghe	01/11/1917	28/11/1917
Operation(al) Order(s)	Operation Order No 26 By Lt Col R.C. Drury., R.F.A. Commanding 50th Divisional Ammn Column.	09/12/1917	09/12/1917
Operation(al) Order(s)	Operation Order No 27 by Lieut Colonel R.C. Drury., R.F.A. Commanding 50th Divisional Ammunition Column.	14/12/1917	14/12/1917
Operation(al) Order(s)	Operation Order No 28 (Part 1) by Lieut Colonel R.C. Drury., RFA Commanding 50th Divisional Ammunition Column.	20/12/1917	20/12/1917
Operation(al) Order(s)	Operation Order No 28 (Part II) by Lieut Col R.C. Drury., R.F.A. Commanding 50th Divisional Ammunition Column.	21/12/1917	21/12/1917
Heading	War Diary of 50th Divisional Ammunition Column. From 1.1.18 To 31.1.18 Volume No. XXXIV.		
War Diary	Vlamertinghe	01/01/1918	08/01/1918
War Diary	Poperinghe	09/01/1918	10/01/1918
War Diary	Guderzeele	13/01/1918	13/01/1918
War Diary	Renescure.	14/01/1918	14/01/1918
War Diary	Merck St Lievin	15/01/1918	31/01/1918
Operation(al) Order(s)	Operation Order No 31 by Lieut Colonel R.C. Drury, R.F.A. Commanding 50th Divisional Ammunition Column.	27/01/1918	27/01/1918
Operation(al) Order(s)	Operation Order No 35 by Lieut Colonel R.C. Drury. R.F.A. Commanding 50th Divisional Ammunition Column.	28/01/1918	28/01/1918
Operation(al) Order(s)	Operation Order No 36 By Lieut Colonel R.C. Drury. R.F.A. Commanding 50th Divisional Ammunition Column.	29/01/1918	29/01/1918
Miscellaneous	Table Referred To		
Operation(al) Order(s)	Operation Order No 33 by Lieut Colnel R.C. Drury., R.F.A. Commanding 50th Divisional Ammunition Column.	26/01/1918	26/01/1918
Operation(al) Order(s)	Operation Order No 32 by Lieut Col R.C. Drury., R.F.A. Commanding 50th Divisional Ammunition Column. For 15th January. 1918.	14/01/1918	14/01/1918
Operation(al) Order(s)	Operation Order No 31 by Lieut Col R.C. Drury., R.F.A. Commanding 50th Divisional Ammunition Column. For 14.1.18.	13/01/1918	13/01/1918
Operation(al) Order(s)	Operation Order No 30 by Lieut Colonel R.C. Drury., R.F.A. Commanding 50th Divisional Ammunition Column.	12/01/1918	12/01/1918
Operation(al) Order(s)	Operation Order No 29 by Lieut Colonel R.C. Drury., R.F.A. Commanding 50th Divisional Ammunition Column.	07/01/1918	07/01/1918
Miscellaneous	Map Locations referred to		
Heading	War Diary Of 50th Divisional Ammunition Column From 1-2-18 To 28-2-18 Volume No XXXIV		
War Diary	Vlamertinghe	01/02/1918	28/02/1918
Operation(al) Order(s)	Operation Order No 38 By Lieut Colonel R.C. Drury., R.F.A. Commanding 50th Divisional Ammunition Column.	24/02/1918	24/02/1918

Operation(al) Order(s)	Operation Order No 37 By Lieut Colonel R.C. Drury., R.F.A. Commanding 50th Divisional Ammunition Column.	20/02/1918	20/02/1918
Operation(al) Order(s)	Operation Order No. 39 by Lieut Colonel R.C. Drury., R.F.A. Commanding 50th Divisional Ammunition Column.	24/02/1918	24/02/1918
Heading	50th (Northumbrian) Divisional Artillery. 50th Divisional Ammunition Column R.F.A. March 1918		
War Diary	Merck St Lievin	01/03/1918	10/03/1918
War Diary	Beataucourt	12/03/1918	12/03/1918
War Diary	Cappy	15/03/1918	15/03/1918
War Diary	Brusle	16/03/1918	21/03/1918
War Diary	Buire	22/03/1918	22/03/1918
War Diary	Villers-Carbonnel	23/03/1918	23/03/1918
War Diary	Diencourt	24/03/1918	24/03/1918
War Diary	Cappy	25/03/1918	25/03/1918
War Diary	Proyart	25/03/1918	25/03/1918
War Diary	Marcelcave	26/03/1918	31/03/1918
Operation(al) Order(s)	Operation Order No 40 By Captain H.L. Meagher. R.F.A. Commanding 50th Divisional Ammunition Column.	08/03/1918	08/03/1918
Operation(al) Order(s)	Operation No 42 By Captain H.L. Meagher. R.F.A. Commanding 50th Divisional Ammunition Column.	11/03/1918	11/03/1918
Operation(al) Order(s)	Operation Order No 43 By Captain H.L. Meagher R.F.A. (T). Commanding 50th Divisional Ammunition Column.	15/03/1918	15/03/1918
Heading	50th Divisional Artillery. 50th Divisional Ammunition Column R.F.A. April 1918.		
Heading	War Diary Of 50th Divisional Ammunition Column. From To 1-4-18 30.4.18. Volume XXXVII		
War Diary	Sains En Amienois	01/04/1918	14/04/1918
War Diary	Lapugnoy	15/04/1918	30/04/1918
Operation(al) Order(s)	Operation Order No 40 by Lieut Colonel R.C. Drury. R.F.A. Commanding 50th Divisional Ammunition Column.	27/04/1918	27/04/1918
Operation(al) Order(s)	Operation Order No 45 By Lt. Col. R.C. Drury, Commanding 50 D.A.C.	29/04/1918	29/04/1918
Heading	War Diary Of 50th Divisional Ammunition Column From 1.5.18. To 31.5.18. Volume XXXVIII		
War Diary	Fere en Tardenois	01/05/1918	27/05/1918
War Diary	Glennes	27/05/1918	27/05/1918
War Diary	Dravegny	28/05/1918	31/05/1918
Operation(al) Order(s)	Operation Order No 47 by Lieut Colonel R.C. Drury. R.F.A. Commanding 50th Divisional Ammunition Column.	10/05/1918	10/05/1918
Operation(al) Order(s)	Operation Order No 46 by Lieut Colonel R.C. Drury. R.F.A. Commanding 50th Divisional Ammunition Column.	04/05/1918	04/05/1918
Heading	War Diary Of 50th Divisional Ammunition Column. From 1.6.18 To 30.6.18 Volume XXXIX		
War Diary	Courjeonnet	01/06/1918	30/06/1918
War Diary	Lesepees Fme Lachy		
War Diary	Lachy	01/07/1918	01/07/1918
War Diary	Pleurs	01/07/1918	02/07/1918
War Diary	Lachy	02/07/1918	02/07/1918
War Diary	Mailly	03/07/1918	03/07/1918

War Diary	Fere Champenoise	03/07/1918	03/07/1918
War Diary	Sommesous	03/07/1918	03/07/1918
Operation(al) Order(s)	Operation Order No. 48 By Lieut Colonel R.C. Drury. R.F.A. Commanding 50th Divisional Ammunition Column.	27/07/1918	27/07/1918
War Diary	Mailly	04/07/1918	04/07/1918
War Diary	Fere Champenoise	04/07/1918	04/07/1918
War Diary	Sommesous	04/07/1918	04/07/1918
War Diary	Allery	05/07/1918	28/07/1918
War Diary	Belloy Sur Somme	29/07/1918	02/08/1918
War Diary	Frechencourt	03/08/1918	09/08/1918
War Diary	Bonnay	10/08/1918	10/08/1918
War Diary	Vaux Sur Somme	11/08/1918	27/08/1918
War Diary	Chipilly	28/08/1918	31/08/1918
Heading	War Diary Of 50th Divisional Ammunition Column. For September. 1918 Volume XLI.		
War Diary	Albert	01/09/1918	01/09/1918
War Diary	Famechon	02/09/1918	03/09/1918
War Diary	Arras	05/09/1918	30/09/1918
Heading	War Diary Of 50th Divisional Ammunition Column For October 1918 Volume XLII		
War Diary		01/10/1918	05/10/1918
War Diary	Arras	06/10/1918	07/10/1918
War Diary	Gouy Servins	08/10/1918	10/10/1918
War Diary	Carency	10/10/1918	12/10/1918
War Diary	Frevin	14/10/1918	14/10/1918
War Diary	Capelle	14/10/1918	16/10/1918
War Diary	Templeux Le Fosse	19/10/1918	19/10/1918
War Diary	Beaurevoir	20/10/1918	20/10/1918
War Diary	Maretz	23/10/1918	25/10/1918
War Diary	Montay	26/10/1918	31/10/1918
Operation(al) Order(s)	Operation Order No 51 by Captain J. Dean., RFA., Commanding 50th Divisional Ammunition Column.	06/10/1918	06/10/1918
Operation(al) Order(s)	Operation Order No 52 by Lieut Col R.C. Drury., RFA., Commanding 50th Divisional Ammunition Colum. for Monday. & Tuesday 14/15th October, 1918	13/10/1918	13/10/1918
Operation(al) Order(s)	Operation Order No 53 by Lieut Colonel R.C. Drury., RFA. Commanding 50th Divisional Ammunition Column. for Saturday 19th October, 1918.	19/10/1918	19/10/1918
Heading	War Diary Of 50th Divisional Ammunition Column. For November, 1918. Volume. XLIII. 30th November, 1918.		
War Diary	Le Cateau	03/11/1918	05/11/1918
War Diary	Le Payt Fme	06/11/1918	09/11/1918
War Diary	Hte Noyelles	10/11/1918	11/11/1918
War Diary	Monleau St Vaast	12/11/1918	30/11/1918
Heading	War Diary. Of 50th Divisional Ammunition Column. For December, 1918. Volume XLV		
War Diary	Monceau St Vaast	01/12/1918	29/12/1918
Heading	War Diary Of 50th Divisional Ammunition Column For January, 1919. Volume XLV.		
War Diary	Frasnoy	01/01/1919	31/01/1919
Heading	War Diary Of 50th Divisional Ammunition Column. For February, 1919 Volume. XLVI 28.2.19		
War Diary	Frasnoy	01/02/1919	28/02/1919

Heading	War Diary Of 50th Divisional Ammunition Column. For March 1919 Volume XLVIII		
War Diary	Frasnoy	01/03/1919	31/03/1919
War Diary		17/03/1919	17/03/1919
Heading	War Diary Of 50th Divisional Ammunition Column For April 1919. Volume XLIX 1.5.19		
War Diary	Frasnoy	19/04/1919	20/04/1919
Heading	War Diary of 50th Divisional Ammunition Column For May 1919. Volume XLX. 1-6-1919.		
War Diary	Frasnoy	06/06/1919	30/06/1919
Heading	War Diaries, October. 1918. Vol XLIII 50th Div. Arty.		

WO95/2820
50 Div
Div Ammunition Column
Aug '14 — May '19

(3)

50TH DIVISION

50TH DIVL AMMN COLUMN
1914 AUG 1915-MAY 1919

50th Division

121/6357

3rd Divis'n Bde R.F.A. Amm'n Col'n

Vol I.

5-8-14
31-7-15

Army Form C. 2118.

1 Ammunition Column
3/4 North. By/RFA

WAR DIARY
or
INTELLIGENCE SUMMARY.
(Erase heading not required.)

Instructions regarding War Diaries and Intelligence Summaries are contained in F. S. Regs., Part II. and the Staff Manual respectively. Title pages will be prepared in manuscript.

Place	Date	Hour	Summary of Events and Information	Remarks and references to Appendices
Durham	5-8-14	—	First day mobilisation.	
do.	15 —	—	Mobilisation completed. Marched to Newcastle	
Newcastle	21 —	—	Marched to Ravensworth. Remained in Training until 5-11-14	
Ravensworth	5-11-14	—	Marched to Low Fell. Billeted	
Low Fell	9-11-14	—	Marched to Sunderland area. Coast Defence duty.	
Sunderland area	29-1-15	—	Marched to Low Fell. Billeted	
Low Fell	17-4-15	—	Entrained for Southampton.	
Southampton	18-4-15	—	Embarked.	
Havre	19-4-15	—	Disembarked.	
Havre	20-4-15	—	Entrained	
Hazebrouck	21-4-15	—	Detrained. Marched to Rouge Croix.	

Army Form C. 2118.

2. Ammunition Column
3rd Hull N/y RFA

WAR DIARY
or
INTELLIGENCE SUMMARY.
(Erase heading not required.)

Instructions regarding War Diaries and Intelligence Summaries are contained in F. S. Regs., Part II. and the Staff Manual respectively. Title pages will be prepared in manuscript.

Place	Date	Hour	Summary of Events and Information	Remarks and references to Appendices
Rouge Croix	22-4-15	—	Billeted.	
do	23-4-15	—	Marched Mont de Cats.	
Mont de Cats	24-4-15	—	Marched Rouge Croix.	
Rouge Croix	25-4-15	—	Marched Rattekot.	
Rattekot	26-4-15	—	Marched St Laurent. Small Amm Section detached and marched to Vlamertinghe. Gun Section remained with Brigade. (See attached sheet)	
Vlamertinghe	27-4-15	—	Attached 28th Division. Got into touch with D.L.I. Brigade at Potijze. Remained in touch with D.L.I. Brigade during second battle of Ypres. Until 4-5-15. Marched to Watou.	
Watou	5-5-15		Marched Winnezeele and billeted.	

1577 Wt. W10791/1773 500,000 1/15 D. D. & L. A.D.S.S./Forms/C. 2118.

Army Form C. 2118.

2a Ammunition Column 3rd Anti-Aircraft RFA

WAR DIARY
or
INTELLIGENCE SUMMARY.

(Erase heading not required.)

Place	Date	Hour	Summary of Events and Information	Remarks and references to Appendices
Rattekot	26/4/15		Marched St Gauvent. Billeted	
St Gauvent	27.4.15		Marched Ge Seuple. Billeted } Gun Section	
Ge Seuple	6-5-15		Marched Winnezeele and rejoined Small Arm Section. Billeted	

Army Form C. 2118.

B. Runnington Brown

3rd N.M. Bty. RFA

WAR DIARY
or
INTELLIGENCE SUMMARY.
(Erase heading not required.)

Instructions regarding War Diaries and Intelligence Summaries are contained in F. S. Regs., Part II. and the Staff Manual respectively. Title pages will be prepared in manuscript.

Place	Date	Hour	Summary of Events and Information	Remarks and references to Appendices
Winnezeele	10-5-15		Marched Watou. Billeted.	
Watou	13-5-15		Small Arm Section marched G 3 c Ypres area and refurnished Infantry reserve 151st Inf. Bde.	
G 3 c	14-5-15		Returned to refilling point. 1 mile E of Watou. S.A.A. again completed.	
Watou	18-5-15		Small Arm Section marched G.3.c Ypres area and refurnished Infantry reserve 151st Inf. Bde.	
G 3 c	18-5-15		Returned to refilling point. 1 mile E of Watou. S.A.A. again completed.	
Watou	19-5-15		Gun and Small Arm Sections marched to G 12 b Vlamertinghe. Got into touch with Batton in fighting line and with Infantry Reserve.	

1577 Wt. W10791/1773 500,000 1/15 D. D. & L. A.D.S.S./Forms/C. 2118.

Army Form C. 2118.

Crow. Col.
Bdr. Moth. M. RFA

WAR DIARY
or
INTELLIGENCE SUMMARY.
(Erase heading not required.)

Instructions regarding War Diaries and Intelligence Summaries are contained in F.S. Regs., Part II. and the Staff Manual respectively. Title pages will be prepared in manuscript.

Place	Date	Hour	Summary of Events and Information	Remarks and references to Appendices
Sheet B. 36				
B.17.D.2.3.	23/7/15	—	Capt. Abbott went to Hospital 5 p.m. Took command of 2 A.C. Killed at 11th S.A.G.	
do	24/7/15		Supplied Bombs to 150th Infy. Bde H.Qrs. Gun position changed 8.10 to 5.30 a.m. Obtained sanction to move to Super Russell or B.21.A.7.2 and occupied same at 7.30 p.m. Fd. Adamson issued to A.C.	
B.21.A.7.2.	25th		Supplied Bombs to 150th Infy Bde H.Qrs. Supplied 48 rounds with French Howitzer Ammun to Hope. 151st Infy Bde to 23rd Trench Battery. Supplied Rounds and men to Balloon Section. Paid men 5 (in) sub.	
do.	26th.		Supplied Bombs to 150th Infy Bde H.Qrs. In attendance with addition of establishment [illegible] sent to Div. Train 2 Ammun. Col. + 1 H.Qr Staff Reinforced G.S. Wagon partly to horses + 2 mules also complete with harness.	
do	27th		Had A.C. Horses examined by Od-O&O an infected Supplied Bombs to 150th Infy Bde H.Qr. Supplied additional Horses + men to Balloon Sec. Inspected by C/Col. + Adjt.	

Army Form C. 2118.

Amm: Col
3rd Hull Bde RFA

Instructions regarding War Diaries and Intelligence Summaries are contained in F. S. Regs, Part II. and the Staff Manual respectively. Title pages will be prepared in manuscript.

WAR DIARY
or
INTELLIGENCE SUMMARY.
(Erase heading not required.)

Place	Date	Hour	Summary of Events and Information	Remarks and references to Appendices
B.21.A.7.2.	28 July 15		Supplied Bombs & U.Rifle to 150th Inf. Bde. HQrs - Took Statements of witnesses as ordered in case of Hilda & Hayes.	
do	29th		Supplied Bombs to 150th Inf. Bde. Supplied 80 Rounds to No2 R.M.L. Trench Howitzer Sect. to 2nd Trench Howitzer Battery. Inspected by Col. & Adjt. Rode on	
do	30th		Supplied Bombs to 150th Inf. Bde. Closed road to Armr. Cart to Lt. Adamson. Left Armr Cart, and handed over Armr. Cart to 3rd Battery. Supplied 150th Infantry Bde to be attacked on duty to 3rd Battery. 2nd Lt. Thorburn joined Col. Bde. with 8 boxes S.A.A. at Armentières. Supplied horses and guns to Batteries to Ballon. Lantern. Supplied Bombs & Gas helmets to the 150th Inf Bde at Armentières.	
do	31			
do	2 Aug 15		Supplied horses and reserve horses Supplied Bombs to 150th to forming up of Rifle Leopfields. Bdr. to to the 150th Inf. Bdr. No 6 Company Stables. Inspected by O.C. Bde. Supplied 150th Inf Batn in R.84/GO S.F.A. and Howitzer Bty to the 150th Inf Bde and Armentières.	

D/
63444

50th Division

60th Div: Ammn Col

Vol I

20-11-14 Jne
31- 7- 15 Jne

Aug 15
Nov 15

Page 1, Vol 1

Army Form C. 2118.

WAR DIARY
or
INTELLIGENCE SUMMARY.
(Erase heading not required.)

Place	Date	Hour	Summary of Events and Information	Remarks and references to Appendices
Cocken Hall nr. Durham	20/11/14		The Northumbrian Divisional Ammunition Column was formed by men drawn from the 3rd and 4th Northumbrian (County of Durham) Reserve Brigades R.F.A. the 1st Northumbrian (Northumberland) and the 2nd Northumbrian (East Riding of Yorks) Brigades R.F.A. being unable to supply the proportion of men required from them. The Unit, under the command of Hon. Col. F.W. Clayff, consisted of 4 sections. Three of these were divided into Gun and S.A.A. Subsections, the 4th into Howitzer and Heavy Battery subsections. These Sections were allotted as follows. 1st Section to supply 1st Northumbrian Brigade Ammunition Column. 2nd Do Do Do 3rd Do Do Do 3rd Do Do Do	

Page 2 Ovt 2

Army Form C. 2118.

WAR DIARY
or
INTELLIGENCE SUMMARY.
(Erase heading not required.)

Place	Date	Hour	Summary of Events and Information	Remarks and references to Appendices
	20/11/14 to 8/1/15		4th Section to supply the 4th Northumbrian Brigade Ammunition Column fourteen and the North Riding Yorks. Heavy Battery. Foot drill, Marching drill, Physical drill and signalling were daily carried out, no other means of training gunners or drivers being available.	
	9/1/15		Arrived at Newcastle on Tyne. NEWCASTLE on TYNE Sections attached to their respective Brigades for training.	
	10/1/15		War Establishments (Reprinted with amendments 5 Feb 3/15) received, altering the establishment of this unit by substituting L.D. horses per G.L. wagon instead of 4 H.D. horses, 75 more drivers now being required, and taking away the Heavy Battery subsection from the 4th section, this subsection now becoming Corps troops	
	6/4/15			

Page 3. Vol 1.

Army Form C. 2118.

WAR DIARY
or
INTELLIGENCE SUMMARY.
(Erase heading not required.)

Place	Date	Hour	Summary of Events and Information	Remarks and references to Appendices
Newcastle on Tyne	10/4/15		Arrived at Park Royal Willesden. to be fitted out for Service overseas, the carrying out of which was greatly facilitated by the very able supervision of Lt Col. R.L. Prior.	
Park Royal	15/4/15		Received 504 mules in place of L.D. horses, and 47 riding horses.	
	16/4/15		United War Office to report that 52 drivers were still required to complete new Establishment and that the Unit was under orders to proceed abroad on the 18th April.	
	17/4/15		Ordered to remain at Park Royal pending the completion of Establishment.	
	20/4/15		Received draft of 52 drivers from the Northumbrian Brigade all entrained to PARK ROYAL.	
	22/4/15		Left PARK ROYAL for Southampton SOUTHAMPTON.	
	23/4/15		Arrived at HAVRE and entrained for HAZEBROUCK (Short 27 Belgium part of France)	

Page 4. Vol 1.

WAR DIARY
or
INTELLIGENCE SUMMARY

Army Form C. 2118.

Place	Date	Hour	Summary of Events and Information	Remarks and references to Appendices
	24/4/15		Arrived at ~~Borre~~ BORRE, Sheet 27 W15a. WATOU Sheet 27 south	
	25/4/15		Ordered to move to a point 2¾ miles east of ~~Watou~~ L.14.c. a distance of 7 kilometres. This led to endless enquiries and was not completed until 11 a.m. on the following day. The wagons being stopped all along the route and a great many men in the ditches. An opportunity should have been given for the training of the personnel, a large number of the drivers had never been mounted before the fitting of harness, which was made for H.D. horses had galls being too short, and the training of mules for draft, to which they were entirely unaccustomed. The large proportion of mules were also unshod on the fore feet.	
	26/4/15		Ordered to move to north of CASTRE (Sheet 27. Q.20.c. Weather March was explicit & unable improved.	

Page 5. Vol 1.

WAR DIARY

INTELLIGENCE SUMMARY

Army Form C. 2118.

Place	Date	Hour	Summary of Events and Information	Remarks and references to Appendices
	27/4/15		d ESTRE (Sheet 27 W.3.a.) Ordered to move to Caestre, a further improvement in march discipline.	
	28/4/15		TERDEGHEM (Sheet 27. J.10.a) Ordered to move to Terdeghem. March discipline very much improved. Having that the Unit moved probably remain here for some little time the training, even the training, training, and shoeing of mules, and the attention of drivers was carried out at high pressure with the result that the Unit was reported mobile and able to supply ammunition within a week of its arrival here. (Sheet 27 K.7.6.)	
	14/5/15		Ordered to move to the point kilometre near WATOU	
	29/9/15		Ordered to take over Hand Grenades Bombs to supply Brigade with same	
	4/10/15		Ordered to move to area east of ABEL (Sheet 27 L.36.c.	

Page 6. Vol 1.

WAR DIARY
or
INTELLIGENCE SUMMARY

Army Form C. 2118.

Place	Date	Hour	Summary of Events and Information	Remarks and references to Appendices
	23/6/15		Ordered to move to CROIX de POPERINGHE (Ouest de Poperinghe) (Sheet 28.M.32.b.)	
	29/7/15		Do NIEPPE	
	3/7/15		Unit still remain at NIEPPE	

121/54/25

50th Division

2nd Northumbrian Bde RFA Amm" Col"

Vol I. 18.4. — 31.5.15.

a2
256

CONFIDENTIAL

War Diary of. 2e. 2: Northumbrian Am. Cd.

Vol. I.

From. 18.4.15   To 31.5.15.

WAR DIARY
or
INTELLIGENCE SUMMARY.   2nd Wm Am Col.

(Erase heading not required.)

Army Form C. 2118.

Hour, Date, Place	Summary of Events and Information	Remarks and references to Appendices
10.20 pm 18/4/15 Newcastle	Entrained & forth Cattle dock (Nelson R Soct.) & two horse (L Soct.) & Stretch	Ry. arrangements Good. A.C.I. in two Trains, for Southn. Provision made for feeding horses en route.
8 AM 19/4/15 Southampton	All horses entrained with harness on. Harness horses only came to hand at the last moment. Arrived & disembarked, stores & horse vehicles, under direction of R.T. Officer. Harness showed much deterioration Sinat. Embarked Officers Split. C.I. C.I. up pending vehicle to ne Transport & horses to another. Breaking up the Sub Sections causing myrics & confusion re equipment &. 10 horses cast - Triplaced. Transports Sailed Hotawa.	2. Man Am. C.I. Officers who embarked. + W. Saunders Capt. + C. Macnamara Lieut. L.R. Williams 2 Lieut A.W.S. Macmillan 2 "
5 pm 19/4/15 Southampton		
Noon 20/4/15 Havre	Entered the dock, & commenced to disembark. By T. Officers great assistance. 3 Q.S. Wagons with horses attached to H.R. Battery for obtaining fourgon.	

WAR DIARY
or
INTELLIGENCE SUMMARY.
(Erase heading not required.)

Army Form C. 2118.

Hour, Date, Place	Summary of Events and Information	Remarks and references to Appendices
20/4/15 Veurne	Sea Plane read from distance but they were unable to supply a large quantity of straw needed for 15 for 43 L.C. guns. Three horse cart replaced.	
10 pm 21/4/15 Hazebrouck	Entrained in left train 2 A.M. 21/4/15. Men accommodated in covered trucks on straw. Horses accommodated 4 aside with centre gangway. 2 men horses in centre alleyway. Stopped for watering down at various intervals. One man left behind - about without kit, sent on Rail. Arrived Hazebrouck in dark. No lights permitted. Resumed men horses + wagons in conjunction. Station put to Sgt a Staff for storage of— 11/15 pm O.C. A.S.C. went ahead to arrange Billets.	
3.30 AM 22/4/15 Staple	Arrived + parked in the Square. Resting horses + distribute horses all day. Start from Billets.	

Forms/C. 2118/10

Army Form C. 2118.

WAR DIARY
or
INTELLIGENCE SUMMARY.
(Erase heading not required.)

Instructions regarding War Diaries and Intelligence Summaries are contained in F.S. Regs., Part II. and the Staff Manual respectively. Title pages will be prepared in manuscript.

Hour, Date, Place		Summary of Events and Information	Remarks and references to Appendices
7 pm	Friday 23/ 4/15 Strazeele	Moved out to support 1" line; proceeded to GODEWERSVELDE to A.G.H. in a band but remained lee of men: BESCATS	passed
2 p.m.	Sat. 24/4/15	Moved back to STRAZEELE	
6.30 p.m.	"	ordered to proceed to WATOU	
2 A.M.	Sun 25/ 4/15 Watou	Arrived at WATOU	
4 A.M.	26/4/15	2 S.t. Macmillan & 7 L. Wagons 2 G.S. wagons at A.S.C. Hqrs- under orders to report hourly. Ready to Acquatic's Canadian lorries at BRIELEN	with S.A.Ammunition
5. P.M.	26 "	Sgt. Watson & W. of WATOU Arrived at new billet	
7 "	"	2 St. L.R.Williams & party left with 4 9.S. wagons S.A.Ammunition under instructions to join 2/LAUS.MacMillan's	
10 "	"	Sup. Column in neighbourhood of BRIELEN.	

Army Form C. 2118.

WAR DIARY
or
INTELLIGENCE SUMMARY.
(Erase heading not required.)

Instructions regarding War Diaries and Intelligence Summaries are contained in F.S. Regs., Part II. and the Staff Manual respectively. Title pages will be prepared in manuscript.

Hour, Date, Place			Summary of Events and Information	Remarks and references to Appendices
27/4/15		WATOU	A.S1 Consists 1 q Ammunition Section only. Exercising & care of Horses Harness.	
6 P.M.	"		Left for WINNEZEELE to take up new Billets	
6 "	28/4/15	WINNEZEELE	Arrived @ new Billets ½ Mile NE. of Village. Parked under Shelter of Trees & Hedges.	Northumbrian Div[isio]n Concentrating round WINNEZEELE.
	29/4/15	"	In daily communication with S.A.A. Section behind firing line supplying ammunition to 1/t 6 Bde — R. Section Early Services Inn Horses. Finding horses in Gun Land.	
	30/4/15	"	Resting & conditioning men & horses. Farriers busy all day re shoeing horses. Drivers & officers attending to harness &c.	

Forms/C. 2118/10

Army Form C. 2118.

WAR DIARY
or
INTELLIGENCE SUMMARY.
(Erase heading not required.)

Instructions regarding War Diaries and Intelligence Summaries are contained in F. S. Regs., Part II. and the Staff Manual respectively. Title pages will be prepared in manuscript.

Hour, Date, Place	Summary of Events and Information	Remarks and references to Appendices
Sat 1/5/15 WINNEZEELE	Visit from Major Gen. Sir W. F. LINDSAY, KCB, b.s.o. Tarpaulin Belts & Wash places freed up.	Com. Hutchen. Bir.
2/5/15 "	Daily Routine duties. Men & Horses daily improving. Branding new horses rec'd ex Southampton & Étaps.	
3/5/15 "	"	
4/5/15 "	Orders rec'd to L. Sec. Am. Co. to return to 2nd Hen A.C.	R Gosier
Midnight 5/5/15 "	L. Sec. arrived at Winnezeele & parked with R. Gosier. Gun drill for Gunners began, sent mar. daily — Men & Horses of L. Sec. returned much exhausted	
6/5/15 "	Extra care & attention given to L. Sec. Horses. Water orders from Vet. Officer.	Hulatter
7/5/15 "	Men & Horses recovering strength fast — with Rest & Feed in Green land —	

WAR DIARY
or
INTELLIGENCE SUMMARY.
(Erase heading not required.)

Army Form C. 2118.

Instructions regarding War Diaries and Intelligence Summaries are contained in F.S. Regs., Part II. and the Staff Manual respectively. Title pages will be prepared in manuscript.

Hour, Date, Place	Summary of Events and Information	Remarks and references to Appendices
8/5/15 @ Winnezeele	Rec. orders to stand bye. half tr. 4 Yukon, 33000 R.t. 4 Yukon 48000 R & S.A.	
9/5/15 "	Stand bye continued. Stand. gr. Stores transport & equipments expenditure	
" "	" orders to be ready to move off at C 30.	
AM 8.30 10/5/15 "	Struck camp & proceeded to A/Q Hn - Tn- Bergen.	
" 11.0 " Hd. Qn ln Bergen	Arr. at S/H in Bergen	
" 11/5/15 "	Routine. received wagon from Army Corps.	
" 12/5/15 "	Resume. Heavy Rain, cold Northerly Wind. Rec. by. motor lorr from N. Am Cot Park 12000 Rds of S.A.A. (Amn Reserve RA)	
" 13/5/15 "	Preparing camp for expedition	
" " "	8/b John T 22, died of peritonitis	
" " "	Rec. orders to be ready to move off at 6.30 p.m.	
7.30 pm " "	Moved off. Rain + N.Wind continued, S. Baggage Wagon from Billeau + Medical Cart attached 10.45 pm. Rec. and wait park nr Q.4	
Midnight " C/S/ G.4. on Poperinghe - Wernudinghe Road.	Passed Hd. A.Q.J. in a field on the R.of to POPERINGHE - VLAMERTINGHE Road. G.4. entrance by Shrine Red Maps Belgium Sheet 28 NW.	
	Left. Battery of N.B.A. St-Jean les Ptseyen	
	sent 2 " to Hqrs 2n Can Artillery	
	1 " to A/Q NY of RSA	
	" 3 Battern of Wess N Line Hd. qrs W. Francis NE of YPRES	

Forms/C. 2118/10

Army Form C. 2118.

WAR DIARY
or
INTELLIGENCE SUMMARY.
(Erase heading not required.)

Instructions regarding War Diaries and Intelligence Summaries are contained in F.S. Regs., Part II. and the Staff Manual respectively. Title pages will be prepared in manuscript.

Hour, Date, Place	Summary of Events and Information	Remarks and references to Appendices
14/5/15 Poperinghe Winnezeeghe Road	Routine. Estd 4 tents in N - Screening Camp from Aircraft - Lt Capt Tankey & Capt Southall V.O. took up quarters with Hd Qrs Col.	
15/5/15 "	Received Machine Guns + 10,000 Rds of S.A.A. from Ahead on Camps apparent - arrived Wed at 9 o'clock for inspection aimed ??? at 15th R.C.A. Amm. can be obtained for M/G from	
	Routine. Ascertained 1st 15th R.C.A. Amm. can be obtained for M/G from Pres. M.G.A. Park at Steenwoorde. Fine & warm Weather.	
16/5/15 Sunday "	Replaced all orderlies & withdrew 1 from 2E. Bde Ad. H.Q. Bellerain in action - no call for Amm.	
	Routine. Machine Gun & S.A.A. removed by R.E. 11.30 A.M. & Artillery. Met L. Cdr in town	
17/5/15 do	Routine. Applied to him for more limber Waggons @ POPERINGHE for 1 Rifle & 3 M/G Waggons.	
18/5/15 do	Routine. Sent H/Q horse No.2710 to Mul. Veterinary Evacuation to become unable to mentally any more. 5. P.M. Rec Instructions from Deguard to fall in ??? L.R. William to report himself at H.Q. S.A. with horse by 10.15 P.M. Taking up 200 Rds of 15" S.A.	

Forms/C. 2118/10

WAR DIARY
or
INTELLIGENCE SUMMARY.
(Erase heading not required.)

Army Form C. 2118.

Hour, Date, Place	Summary of Events and Information	Remarks and references to Appendices
5. P.M. 18.5.15 POPERINGHE Road	Orders rec. from Adjutant to instruct S.S.C. Macnamara to proceed to VLAMERTINGHE to take over command of R.E. Wagon Lines & Pk. & Robinson Wartela. S. Macnamara proceeded with 6 wheeled wagons with Q. & E. wagon loaded 15 pr. & Ammunition.	
8. P.M. "	Q. & E. wagon left having handed over 300 Rds. Q.A. 2", 1500 R.E. Wagon set having handed over 300 Rds. 18 pr. 2, 22 MW. Belgian G Series.	
3. A.M. 19.5.15 "	road junction J.3.d. 7x6. Rd. Map. 22 NW Belgian G Series. Wired to O.C. h.in. Am. Park. STEENVOORDE for 300 Rds. the same.	
horn. 19.5.15 "	Routine work carried. moved from Lines.	
1. PM "	Capt. Tinsley instructed to O.C. B proceed to Potterie 14 Wk. beyond YPRES.	
10. PM "	St. Major Jn. ken A. Park instructed through Orderly Any. 15th Bm. orders not promptly obeyed. Sent mounted orderly to N.O.A. at Sn Jean K1 MESC and to O.C. h. in. Am. Col. WATOU requesting 300 Rds. Am.	
10.10 PM "	to be sent to same at once.	

Army Form C. 2118.

WAR DIARY
or
INTELLIGENCE SUMMARY.
(Erase heading not required.)

Instructions regarding War Diaries and Intelligence Summaries are contained in F. S. Regs., Part II. and the Staff Manual respectively. Title pages will be prepared in manuscript.

Hour, Date, Place	Summary of Events and Information	Remarks and references to Appendices
4.0 A.M. 20/5/15 Poperinghe Rd G.4. C. in 28 Bde R.W.	Capt Craddock arrived from WATOU with 300 Rds. G.A. 15 pr Bau Maxim	
"	Routine. Wanner Stores coming to hand A.S.C. working well.	
5 p.m.	Paid men.	
21/5/15 "	Routine. Exercise - Lewis bike. Cleaning harness etc. Water cart. Men Known Antennae Garden all Schwer. Water supply only moderate. Replaced ordulis with No A.M.T. 9, 1, 2 & 3 Batteries. Sent up 2 Magnesium Pads to Batteries. Sent to New A.C.I enquiring re. Telescope Rocking Bar sight &c. in Store Gen. Staunton called, enquiring as to amount of gun ordnance.	
"	15 p.m. Spare parts used from ordnance.	

WAR DIARY or INTELLIGENCE SUMMARY

Army Form C. 2118.

(Erase heading not required.)

Hour, Date, Place	Summary of Events and Information	Remarks and references to Appendices
22/3/16 Poperinghe VLAMERTINGHE ROAD	Warm & fine. Routine. Wheels greased & turns supplied (Spare Lewis & gun fittings). Enquiries for two H.E.I. Vickers Gun parts (to be sent to Cap. Robinson armr. Corpstre Schools on 23rd)	
23/3/16 "	Routine. Horses leaving the Battalion changed from Lewis. Changed two Lewis gun Wgn. Lmbrs. Mounted orderly arrived with urgent demand for 15 pr. Gun Ammunition — the Sub. to Wgn Lmbr. N.4 VLAMERTINGHE & returned. 17 Rounds	
6.10 AM 24/3/16 "	Sent White 1/R. Scots a number Br. No R. armourers & Board.	BE. A Sergeant armourers &
6.45 " "	Victims Commanding continued. Sent Mk. Cyclop. to Lu A.C1. 01-E.WA 700 for refill	
6.50 " "	Rec. from Gm H.Cl. Shipps 1273 Cartvsn. drgm. 1272.	
10. " "	Total 12.50.	
" "	2.1h no Return reported heavy Enemy from own gun.	
9 " "	Sent 12 addl German to Wgn hrs to Conestua. Working with 12 fit. from Gun castin R.E. gunners.	

WAR DIARY
or
INTELLIGENCE SUMMARY.
(Erase heading not required.)

Army Form C. 2118.

Instructions regarding War Diaries and Intelligence Summaries are contained in F.S. Regs., Part II. and the Staff Manual respectively. Title pages will be prepared in manuscript.

Hour, Date, Place	Summary of Events and Information	Remarks and references to Appendices
Continued		
9.45 AM 24/5/15 Boesinghe Vlamertinghe Road	Sent Motor despatch rider to N.10.A. St. JEAN & BIEZEN advising them of its position & that move ammunition would probably be required.	
10.20 "	Recd. instructions from N.D.A. that I passed I might apply to the 3rd. Div. Am. Col. for ammunition.	
1.10 pm "	Cannonading seemed to be slackening off.	
5.0 " "	Despatch marked urgent from N.D.A. recd. sent forward to O.C. 13th. Bde (2 h'rs R.H.A) as instructed by mounted orderly who also carried a Report from O.C. 2nd. Hb. A. Col.	

WAR DIARY
or
INTELLIGENCE SUMMARY.
(Erase heading not required.)

Army Form C. 2118.

Hour, Date, Place	Summary of Events and Information	Remarks and references to Appendices
24/5/15 Poperinghe Vlamertinghe Rd.	Continued	
6 p.m. "	Capt. Robinson arrived in motor Car in charge of Red 4 M. Officer suffering from loss of memory. I sent him on to the train started by same car at once.	
7/15 "	O/c Wagon Line @ VLAMERTINGHE sent messenger for a Carrier Ring & 1 Strap 13th. Has not having any in 13th A.C. Sent to len A.C.d who supplied Wagon Line using M/cr dis patch rider. I sent for Lt. Macmillan returned from Wagon Line reporting 2/Lt Macmillan has given orders that 6 A.C.d, 7 S 28 Guns, & Capt has given orders that 6 A.C.d to remain at Wagon Line. Wynn was to remain at Wagon Line to see be kept loaded until further orders.	

Army Form C. 2118.

WAR DIARY
or
INTELLIGENCE SUMMARY.
(Erase heading not required.)

Hour, Date, Place	Summary of Events and Information	Remarks and references to Appendices

25.5.15 Popenide Hannahayi Hud

Routine.
Weather fine & hot.

10.0 A.M.

Gen Fanshaw called to enquire re amount of ammunition supplied Turks on the 24.5.15.
It was thinking badly changed from watering by buckets to mod, ammunition boxes with man submerged with.
2 Lieut. four. Am. Col. delivered. 56 Rounds of 15" R.L.E.
Cordite Cartridges.

5 PM

6 G.S. Gun am. Wagons ret'd. Gun wagon Kmr. with
3 Batteries + A. Wheelin g 2 hh Bde R.F.A.
Supplies S.A.A. with. 36,000 Rds. S.A.A. Mk VII.
Visit from Major & Staff Capt. So am
Re: Submimming orders to strike Camp.
Rendim.

10.15 AM 26/5/15 "
Turn Huft.

2.45 " "

Army Form C. 2118.

WAR DIARY
or
INTELLIGENCE SUMMARY.
(Erase heading not required.)

Instructions regarding War Diaries and Intelligence Summaries are contained in F.S. Regs., Part II. and the Staff Manual respectively. Title pages will be prepared in manuscript.

Hour, Date, Place	Summary of Events and Information	Remarks and references to Appendices
29 May Poperinghe VLAMERTINGHE ROAD	Weather fine.	
9 A.M.	Supplied L/Works with 16,000 R.D. S.A.A. Mk VII	
	" " S. M.L.D. " 100,000 "	
12.5 noon	" " orderly sent to 2 Sect. 10 A.C.I. for 100,000 R.D.	
1-20 pm	Rec'd 99 Boxes = 99,000 R.D. from 10 A.C.I.	
	Routine.	
	Preparing wagons for departure.	
4 PM	Left Camp for St. Jean in BIEZEN.	
9.30 " S. Jn. In BIEZEN	Passed 1. Bde. 65 hrs R.F.A. leaving St. Jean L 7.51525M	
9.45	Bivouaced Billet – ½ mile South of S. Jn. Br. in BIEZEN	
	Ref map Hazebrouck Sheet, 5A.	
	Left Sect. (8.H.R.) Remained in Camp on POPERINGHE – VLAMERTINGHE ROAD under 2 Lt A.W. Macmillan. to continue to supply 150 Brit. Bde.	

Forms/C. 2118/10

Army Form C. 2118.

WAR DIARY
or
INTELLIGENCE SUMMARY.
(Erase heading not required.)

Instructions regarding War Diaries and Intelligence Summaries are contained in F. S. Regs., Part II. and the Staff Manual respectively. Title pages will be prepared in manuscript.

Hour, Date, Place	Summary of Events and Information	Remarks and references to Appendices
29/6/15 5-7pm BIEZEN	Rendezvous. Riding School. Cavalry from BAILLEUL. Weather fine (?)	
10 PM " "	Reported to O.C. this AM 60 titlement having Spares. Gun stores in a Set. to H.Q. also date when Gun Limbs had been manded for.	
30/6/15 " "	Rendezvous. Weather fine. Cool. Reported necessity Govt Asst. Blue panels with a Wets Cost. They did Flag X amp; Churchstairs.	
9 A.M. " "		
31/6/15 9 A.M. " "	Left St Jans Ler BIEZEN for ABEELE with whole R. Sect.	
11.15 AM " ABEELE	Grip at ABEELE taking up Billets at point 4 mandis SW Hosp. GODEWAERSVELDE St.	

Army Form C. 2118.

WAR DIARY
or
INTELLIGENCE SUMMARY.
(Erase heading not required.)

Instructions regarding War Diaries and Intelligence Summaries are contained in F.S. Regs., Part II. and the Staff Manual respectively. Title pages will be prepared in manuscript.

Hour, Date, Place	Summary of Events and Information	Remarks and references to Appendices
31/6/17 ABEELE		
10:30 AM	Gained H.Q was also O/C L. Coss stores to the R.E.	
	of him position.	
	Routine.	
	Watering of Inspection.	
	Machine Gun Wagon.	
		H Amato
		Capt OC M.G

Forms/C. 2118/10

137/6763

a2
a96

50th Division

2nd Northumbrian Bde: Ammn Coln

Vol II 1 — 30.6.15.

CONFIDENTIAL

2nd NORTHUMBRIAN BDE.
AMM. COLUMN

WAR DIARY

1/30. JUNE 1915

CAPT. H.W.SMALES. R.F.A.

VOL II

Army Form C. 2118.

WAR DIARY
or
INTELLIGENCE SUMMARY.
(Erase heading not required.)

Instructions regarding War Diaries and Intelligence Summaries are contained in F. S. Regs., Part II. and the Staff Manual respectively. Title pages will be prepared in manuscript.

Place	Date	Hour	Summary of Events and Information	Remarks and references to Appendices
ABEELE	1/6/15	9.0 AM	Left St. JEAN Ter BIEZEN. The A.C.A Consisting of Right Sect. only.	
		11.15	Arr'd ABEELE. Parked the wagons back up how lines at a farm on Leftside of ABEELE – POPERINGHE Road. & ½ mile from ABEELE at point 4 just south	
			of just E. in HILLHOCK. Ref Map. HAZEBROUCK S.A.	
		Noon	Sent out orderlies advising position to H/4 & 1, 2 & 3 Batteries also to A.E.V.	
	2/6/15		Routine, Riding School. "	
	3/6/15		Routine " " "	
		Noon	Lt. M⁰Intyre R.A.M.C gave instruction in use of Respirators.	
	4/6/15	9.0 AM	Capt. Stebelt Inspector of Transport examined all horses & harness jittings, giving instruction in Shoeing + harness fitting – Inspecting Forage + arrangements for storing + Watering – Ending up with a lecture to all Officer NCOs + Routine – Riding School to	

Army Form C. 2118.

Instructions regarding War Diaries and Intelligence Summaries are contained in F. S. Regs., Part II. and the Staff Manual respectively. Title pages will be prepared in manuscript.

WAR DIARY
or
INTELLIGENCE SUMMARY.
(Erase heading not required.)

Place	Date	Hour	Summary of Events and Information	Remarks and references to Appendices
	Jun 4	5 PM	S. Genl. Plumer Commander 2nd Army. visited the lines closely inspecting them which men were being exposed himself as well. General with met he had seen.	
		6.20 PM	Left Billets Hazebrouck Bivouac BOESCHEPE.	
		8.0 "	Arrived at new Billets 1 mile due N. of the town of BOESCHEPE Ref. Map HAZEBROUCK 5A	
BOESCHEPE	" 5		Routine.	
"	" 6	4 AM	Sent Trans. out to Camp 1, B. Sub Sect M. 21. c. 18 Ref. Map 28 & reported new position & O/C the sector.	
"		5 "	Am our orders to report my new position to H/q. D.A.D.S. tele. cable/Tele	
			Routine. Return School Co. Ordence Repairs. Regl. Inspection	
"	" 7	1 AM	"B" Sub. Sect. arrived from Forward Depot.	

Army Form C. 2118.

WAR DIARY
or
INTELLIGENCE SUMMARY.
(Erase heading not required.)

Instructions regarding War Diaries and Intelligence Summaries are contained in F. S. Regs., Part II. and the Staff Manual respectively. Title pages will be prepared in manuscript.

Place	Date	Hour	Summary of Events and Information	Remarks and references to Appendices
BOESCHEPE	8/6/15		Routine.	
"	9/6/15		Routine.	
		2:30 PM	All Am Wagns emptied at Felline Sea-Stand. Rec 1100 Rounds 9pr Am 15 pr, 9pr, 2 Sec, 30 6n R.F.	
"	10/6/15		Routine	
"	11/6/15		All from Wagn equipment inspected & deficiencies indented for	
"	12/6/15			
"	13/6/15		Church parade with 1st Bde 11 bn R.F.A.	
BOESCHEPE	14/6/15		Routine. Riding School & his Preparation Samples Helmets issued to to Am. Col. D.E. Water visited the Camps.	

Army Form C. 2118.

WAR DIARY
or
INTELLIGENCE SUMMARY.
(Erase heading not required.)

Instructions regarding War Diaries and Intelligence Summaries are contained in F. S. Regs., Part II. and the Staff Manual respectively. Title pages will be prepared in manuscript.

Place	Date	Hour	Summary of Events and Information	Remarks and references to Appendices
BOESCHEPE	15/6/15	noon	Routine. Orders recd to send Gun Sect. "B" in charge of Lt. C. Macnamara to point G.17.C.5×8. Shelter 28 ft Supply 2 & Riding Battery in Action with Am.	
		1.35 pm	B Sub Sect Complete left for destination as above.	
		2.30 "	Checked all own R.S.runs very closely.	
		3.0 "	Issued to N.Riding Battery 40 Rounds.	
		4.10 "	A spray hose no men brought into the lines to B/4 advised.	
"	16/6/15		Routine. Riding School. & .	
"	17/6/15		Routine " " " Ring worm Reported in lines	
		2.15 pm	Doubtful 5 horses.	
"	18/6/15		Routine 12 horses affected with Ring worm.	
		10.30 AM	moved two lines to isolate Ring worm cases.	

Army Form C. 2118.

WAR DIARY
or
INTELLIGENCE SUMMARY.
(Erase heading not required.)

Instructions regarding War Diaries and Intelligence Summaries are contained in F.S. Regs., Part II. and the Staff Manual respectively. Title pages will be prepared in manuscript.

Place	Date	Hour	Summary of Events and Information	Remarks and references to Appendices
BOIESCHEPE	19/6/15	noon	Routine. 4 mins Rng Wm Cases Westoutre - Sh&s. Macnamara & B.S. set-repatd	
		5.0 PM	Rec orders to Strike Camp on 20/6/15	
	20/6/15		Routine. No fresh cases of Rny Wm	
		8.30	Regtl HQ Bret - Am Col Rg BOESCHEPE	
		11.15	and C/ WESTOUTRE	
		1.30	Interpretr guided A.Col on to VISAINE	
		noon	Halted A.Col in field. Opposite 3" N midlands An Col Billets. Sent out-orderlies to report position 4/15 etc.	
M'VIDAIGNE	21/6/15		Routine. Instructed by S. Off. 46 Bie. to reconnoitre the wagon lines of 1st 3" N Midlan Rgs & to liase with 151 Inf Bde.	
			Took over the branchline to ground vacated by 2 N Mid A.Col. Located the 151 In Rde @ BRANOUTRE. Reg mns orderly time.	
"	22/6/15	8.30 AM	2/L A.W.S. MACMILLAN instructed to proceed to 2 Battery to report himself to OC.	
		5.10 PM.	Issued to 151 Inf Bde. 504 Rds / Verey's , 2214 AM, & 44,000 Rds SAA.	

WAR DIARY
or
INTELLIGENCE SUMMARY.

Army Form C. 2118.

Place	Date	Hour	Summary of Events and Information	Remarks and references to Appendices
M¹ VIBAIGNE	23/6/15		Routine. Heavy overnight Nitrous from Return. Respirators KRyles	
"	24/6/15		Routine. Issued to N.Rday Battery 44 Rd 15 pr Am	
"	25/6/15		Routine. Inspection of Wagon to Gun Spare Stores	
"	26/6/15		Routine. Issued 15,000 Ra SAA. & 15 pr Rd. "1 PRBdE, 42 Rd 15 pr Am. - Repairs dam c/W Truck	
"	27/6/15		Routine. Issued 55,000 Ra SAA & 15 pr Rd 10 -	
"	28/6/15		Routine.	
"	29/6/15		Routine. Issued to N.R Battery 44 Rd 15 pr Am " - L N Lines 20,000 Ra SAA.	

WAR DIARY
INTELLIGENCE SUMMARY

Place	Date	Hour	Summary of Events and Information	Remarks and references to Appendices
MKVISAIGNE	30/10/15		Routine. Issued to Battery. 44 Rds /15 pdr. Prisoners B. GREEN & PAYNE before me for sleeping on piquet. Remanded to O.C. Weather dull. Wind S.	

M. Mitchell
Capt. R.N.V.R. (T)
Comd'g. 2nd N. Zealand Arty. Comd.

121/6356

50th Division

1) 3rd Gotha Rd RFA Amm'n Col'n

Vol III

1-31-7-15

CONFIDENTIAL

WAR DIARY
of
Capt. H. W. Sneden R.F.A.
2 Div. Am. Col.

1 July to 31 July

Vol. III

Army Form C. 2118.

WAR DIARY
or
INTELLIGENCE SUMMARY.
(Erase heading not required.)

Place	Date 1915	Hour	Summary of Events and Information		Remarks and references to Appendices
				Issued.	
				Rounds	
				Gun 15pr S.A.A	
MONT VIDAIGNE	July 1		Routine. All Am: wagon wheels painted with wet grease. Supplying 6 A.M. to 2 NNH 13de R.F.A + 151 Ind Bde.	88 57,000	
"	2		Routine. Inspect of "W.S. Set Hermes" Telephone Instrument taken away.	4,000	
"	3		Routine. Reduction of Establishment of S.A.A. [32) - 200 R.Q. C. + 2 & 9. Wagm. (known as _____)	27,000	
"	4		Routine. Lt. McNamara, forward Obs. Officer for 2 NN No. R.F.A 2 Lt. AW.S. McMillan (shoes identified)	200	
"	5		Routine. Inspecting "C" Sub. Sect.	44 55,000	
"	6		Routine. "Pay day".		

1577 Wt.W10791/1773 500,000 1/15 D.D.&L. A.D.S.S./Forms/C. 2118.

Army Form C. 2118.

WAR DIARY
or
INTELLIGENCE SUMMARY.
(Erase heading not required.)

Instructions regarding War Diaries and Intelligence Summaries are contained in F. S. Regs., Part II. and the Staff Manual respectively. Title pages will be prepared in manuscript.

Place	Date	Hour	Summary of Events and Information	Remarks and references to Appendices
	July			Issued
				Rounds
				Gun no S.A.A
MONT VIDAIGNE	7		Recd 800 Rds 1" dummy standup Am for 25, 7H Rd Bm @ KEMMEL	76
"	8			
"	9		Issue Supplies of new 80" 15 Pr Gun Am.	56 78 20.000
"	10		Ammn to A.R.C. Island posted "New Government" to 6" Gun E.L.	60 88 82 35.000
"	11		Comm trained on b Paper 18 grain stopping above Jumpers Exchanged sub just 4 9.2 wagons 1 old 15" An for New Bc 202	576 124 9.000
"	12			

1577 Wt.W10791/1773 500,000 1/15 D. D. & L. A.D.S.S./Forms/C. 2118.

Army Form C. 2118.

WAR DIARY
or
INTELLIGENCE SUMMARY.
(Erase heading not required.)

Instructions regarding War Diaries and Intelligence Summaries are contained in F. S. Regs., Part II. and the Staff Manual respectively. Title pages will be prepared in manuscript.

Place	Date	Hour	Summary of Events and Information	Remarks and references to Appendices
	1915 July			
MONT VIDAIGNE	13	9 am PM	Routine	48000
"	14		Routine. Propagation proceedings of court martial. Arrow Payne Green recruits since left.	308
"	15		Routine. Health of troops continues excellent.	43 16,000
"	16		Routine	7000
PONT de NIEPPE	17	6 PM 10.0 PM	Routine. Rec orders send 2 O/s Wyum & SAA to 149 Inf Bde left Mt VIDAIGNE for Pont d. NIEPPE arrived 2. AM 18.	
	18		Fixing new Lines in Brick fields. Room mined to adjoining fields.	50,000
	19		Routine	200,000

Army Form C. 2118.

WAR DIARY
or
INTELLIGENCE SUMMARY.
(Erase heading not required.)

Instructions regarding War Diaries and Intelligence Summaries are contained in F. S. Regs., Part II. and the Staff Manual respectively. Title pages will be prepared in manuscript.

Place	Date	Hour	Summary of Events and Information		Remarks and references to Appendices
PONT A NIEPPE	20		Routine		30.000
	21		"		31.000
	22		"		
	23		"	2	
	24		Capt Alexander leaves to rejoin to N.R. Battery formerhunte	79 42	
			Capt W.P. Kerr-Muller takes over Comd of Am. Col.	90	31.000
	25		"		
	26		W.R. Plimer M. Kemp. Champneys to T. Battery.	84	30.000
	27		"		

1577 Wt.W10791/1773 500,000 1/15 D. D. & L. A.D.S.S./Forms/C. 2118.

Army Form C. 2118.

WAR DIARY
or
INTELLIGENCE SUMMARY.
(Erase heading not required.)

Instructions regarding War Diaries and Intelligence Summaries are contained in F. S. Regs., Part II. and the Staff Manual respectively. Title pages will be prepared in manuscript.

Place	Date	Hour	Summary of Events and Information	Remarks and references to Appendices
	July			
Pont du NIEPPE	28		Routine	Guns S/A/A
				108
	29	"	" Which Very Welcome	
				69
	30	"		
	31	"	Month of June Good. Conditions Somewhat Welie Pond Hopeless	108
	Summary		Issues during Month of July	Rifle Grens 143
			Gun Am. S.A.A. Very Lights Grenades Bombers 55-4	
			12" x 12" 682,000 2210	
			Rens. 2471.	
			Rockets Daylight Sigs	
			10 2C.	

A Woodvale
Capt 12th O.H.L.I.

50th Division

1/3
1/8rd Indian Boe Amm" Col"· R+A.

Vol II

From 1 - 31. 8. 15.

50th Division

121/7016

Confidential
War Diary
of
Lieut Colonel F. W. Cluff
50th Divisional Ammunition Column
From 1st August 1915 to 31st August 1915

Volume II

WAR DIARY
or
INTELLIGENCE SUMMARY.
(Erase heading not required.)

Army Form C. 2118.

Places	Date	Hour	Summary of Events and Information	Remarks and references to Appendices
NIEPPE	1/9/15		Still at the same place nothing of note outside ordinary routine work.	
Do	16/9/15		Owing to scarcity of water the Column was ordered to move to a position two miles north of BAILLEUL on the BAILLEUL — BETHUNE Road, the supply of ammunition to the Brigade Ammunition Columns the undertaken by an advanced section of the 50th Divisional Sub-Park	
	17/9/15			
	19/9/15		Further orders received in regard to the above mentioned move to the effect that the Headquarters and section were to remain at NIEPPE, the former to continue the distribution of Bombs Hand Grenades and to generally supervise the ammunition supply. The latter to supply rations for 2nd Army Workshops and the 50th Divisional Engineers. 1st 3rd & 4th Sections moved to new area.	

Army Form C. 2118.

WAR DIARY
or
INTELLIGENCE SUMMARY.
(Erase heading not required.)

Instructions regarding War Diaries and Intelligence Summaries are contained in F. S. Regs., Part II. and the Staff Manual respectively. Title pages will be prepared in manuscript.

Place	Date	Hour	Summary of Events and Information	Remarks and references to Appendices
NIEPPE	28/9/15		The supply of 15 pounder B.L.C. ammunition which from the beginning of July, had been of the new type only, with the 80 fuze in place of the 65 fuze, reverted again to the old pattern, 1050 rounds of this was supplied from which the fuzes of which were of a very mixed character, consisting of a large number of different lots and numbers, and also the numerals of the mean time of burning, in many cases, also being different. In order to avoid the Artillery Brigades having a large number of small lots returns of all 65 fuzes drawing in the different lots thanks dates when called for, in order that the fuzes might be regrouped made up into as large lots of similar markings as possible. The returns showed no less than 55 different lots.	
21/9/16 29/9/15			Nothing of importance to report.	

1577 Wt. W10791/1773 500,000 1/15 D. D. & L. A.D.S.S./Forms/C. 2118.

Army Form C. 2118.

WAR DIARY
or
INTELLIGENCE SUMMARY.
(Erase heading not required.)

Instructions regarding War Diaries and Intelligence Summaries are contained in F. S. Regs., Part II. and the Staff Manual respectively. Title pages will be prepared in manuscript.

Place	Date	Hour	Summary of Events and Information	Remarks and references to Appendices
NIEPPE	30/9/15		Notification received that the Establishment of 15 pounder ammunition both in the Brigade Ammunition Columns and the Divisional Ammunition Column was to be reduced and 72 pounds per gun to be carried in place of 144. The resulting surplus wagons were to be sent back to ABBEVILLE. The Establishment of 5" Howitzer held by the Divisional Ammunition Column was also reduced by one half viz from 92 pounds per gun to 46 pounds per gun.	

121/6857

50th Division

2nd North'n Bde RFA Ammn Colm
Vol X

August 1. 1915

an
a/6

WAR DIARY
or
INTELLIGENCE SUMMARY.
(Erase heading not required.)

Army Form C. 2118

Place	Date	Hour	Summary of Events and Information	Remarks and references to Appendices
PONT du NIEPPE	1/8/17		Routine Officers & Men practised in Billets. Wagon Drivers in their respective Brick fields with Buildings forms.	
	2 Aug		11 Men Gunners attached to E Batteries for Instruction	
	3 "			
	4 "		Capt. H.S. Snooks relieving Gun N.R.13 Battery took over command of 1/15 Capt. W.P. nun Welles returned to H.R. Battery for duty. Sgt Todhunter E (806) & Cpl. Gleed J. No 512 posted to A.E.C.	
	5 "			
	6 "		A Bows:- Fletcher, George Wheeler posted Rounds. Gr. Mustopek, Qwention Lazard leaving Manain posted P. W. Bal.	
	7 "			
	8 "		Church parade - men Horses Fit.	

Army Form C. 2118

WAR DIARY
or
INTELLIGENCE SUMMARY.
(Erase heading not required.)

Instructions regarding War Diaries and Intelligence Summaries are contained in F. S. Regs., Part II. and the Staff Manual respectively. Title pages will be prepared in manuscript.

Place	Date	Hour	Summary of Events and Information	Remarks and references to Appendices
PONT de NIEPPE	Aug 9th		Routine.	
	10		Leaky inspection of Arms, Ammn, Iron Rations+Respirators.	
			Completed painting Wagon Covers + Making Archival Frames Works in Wood + Wattans near Wagons	
	11			
	12		Major 2nd A.D.V.S. instructed H.Q. have rec'd from A.S.C. Isle Pencils Mobile Vet. Sec.	
	13		2 Lt. w.T.O. Bonniwell posted to H.Q. from 2 Sim. (every Friday). N.C.O.s Clerks from 3 to 5. pay day.	
	14		Inspection, A.M. Aux. Sec. / Route March. Attached Officers Visited A.C.H.	
	15		Sunday. Inspection of G.S. Sub. Sec. + Route March. Baillon Camp out of Action.	
	16		Small kit Inspection.	

Army Form C. 2118.

WAR DIARY
or
INTELLIGENCE SUMMARY.
(Erase heading not required.)

Instructions regarding War Diaries and Intelligence Summaries are contained in F. S. Regs., Part II. and the Staff Manual respectively. Title pages will be prepared in manuscript.

Place	Date	Hour	Summary of Events and Information	Remarks and references to Appendices
	August			
	17		Review W.r. 16 then Rt.a from 1 Battery (digging party)	
	18		Sent out E. & Batty. Main purpose. " Changed from line outside to Breastpin a given	
	19		Sub-Sec- Rute made over.	
PONT. NIEPPE	20	9.30 P.M	Left mult R + L Sections for NIEPPE. & parked in field pond 13.21.B.9×10 with Q. Sec: 55 Bn A Co in adjoining field. Water in pond & well very bad, obliged to water @ River	
NIEPPE	21		Routine. Apt. Morley 1 Mody Pt. Previous 1 Mule park. All men paraded in public Watering receptions 6 tr a day. @ River. - Pay day -	
	22		Routine Church parade.	
	23		5 men posted to R. Battier & attend B. G. Sig. Wilting Classes.	
	24		Corp Burke Bowen on leave. Maj. Watman takes Command of 10% absence of O/c on leave	

1577 Wt. W10791/1773 500,000 1/15 D. D. & L. A.D.S.S./Forms/C. 2118.

Army Form C. 2118.

WAR DIARY
or
INTELLIGENCE SUMMARY.
(Erase heading not required.)

Instructions regarding War Diaries and Intelligence Summaries are contained in F. S. Regs., Part II. and the Staff Manual respectively. Title pages will be prepared in manuscript.

Place	Date	Hour	Summary of Events and Information	Remarks and references to Appendices
NIEPPE	August 25		Routine. Very hot & clear	
	26		Orders received to supply 1 & 2 R.F. Battery with 30 rnds Gun Am. Requisitions for above sent to Minden for fresh standings	
	27		Prisoner before O.C. Pay day.	
	28		Water scarce, wagons sent to get fresh draws with nightmen from Sunk Well Dupan	
	29		Church parade	
	30		Rode to Mt Noir to see Capt. Southill in hospital — Reading Breaks — for horse standings from Chapelle Armoutier	
	31		Reading Bricks for horse standings. Ammunition issued during the Month	

	15-pdr Shell how	S.A.A.	Verylight	Rocket Riflegun	Hand grenade
	992 1548	352,000	1440	60	85 131
	2740				
		Pistol Am, 208			

[Signature]
CAPT. R.F.A. (T)
COMD'G. 2ND NIGERIAN AMM. COL.

121/6918

50th Division

2nd North'n Bde RFA Amm'n Col

Vol III

Sept. 15.

Army Form C. 2118

WAR DIARY
or
INTELLIGENCE SUMMARY.
(Erase heading not required.)

Instructions regarding War Diaries and Intelligence Summaries are contained in F.S. Regs., Part II. and the Staff Manual respectively. Title pages will be prepared in manuscript.

Place	Date	Hour	Summary of Events and Information	Remarks and references to Appendices
NIEPPE	1/9/15	8 a.m.	1 N.C.O, 12 drivers + 6 brakesmen left with 6 G.S. wagons (Gun section) for A.T. depot RA section. Wagons struck off strength	CRC
	2/9/15		Supplied ammunition to 150th Bde.	CRC
	4/9/15		20 men rejoined from H.Q.S	CRC
	5/9/15		Supplied S.A.A to 150th Bde.	CRC
	7/9/15	6.30 a.m	12 men left for 14 days Gun laying instruction in exchange for 12 from batteries.	CRC
		5.30 p.m	3 G.S wagons drew 3000 bricks from Chapelle d'Armentières for stables	
	8/9/15		Supplied SAA to 150th & 13 Bde.	CRC
	10/9/15		1 CNC.O + 5 brakesmen returned, one left in Hospital, drivers returned at A.T. depot.	CRC
	11/9/15		Supplied SAA to 150th & 151st Bde.	C&C
	12/9/15		" " 149th Bde. "B" SAA only to be issued for machine guns.	CRC
	13/9/15	5.30 a.m	Started with 6 G.S. wagons to draw bricks (39,000) from Chapelle d'Armentières for stables. Supplied SAA to 150th & 151st Bde.	CRC
	14/9/15	7 a.m	6 G S wagons started for Mont Noir to draw sand for stables.	CRC
		5.30 p.m	6 G S wagons started for Chapelle d'Armentières for bricks (only to be drawn at night) Supplied SAA to 151, 2nd Bde. LT. ADAMSON PROCEEDED on leave	
	15/9/15	8 a m	4 G S wagons sent to 3rd Battery to draw bricks 2 G S " " " M Nout Noir for 3rd Batt.	CRC

Army Form C. 2118.

WAR DIARY
or
INTELLIGENCE SUMMARY.
(Erase heading not required.)

Instructions regarding War Diaries and Intelligence Summaries are contained in F. S. Regs., Part II. and the Staff Manual respectively. Title pages will be prepared in manuscript.

Place	Date	Hour	Summary of Events and Information	Remarks and references to Appendices
MEPPE	15/9/15		Drew bricks from CHAPELLE D'ARMENTIÈRE. Supplied 151st Bde with S.A.A.	
			"U" S.A.A. returned to base	
	16/9/15		Supplied wagons + drew sand for 3rd Battery. Drew bricks at night.	
			Supplied S.A.A. to 151st Bde	
	17/9/15		Supplied wagons + drew sand for 3rd Batt. Drew bricks at night. Supplied S.A.A. to 151st Bde. Built Observing Station in line for 2nd G.H.Q. line.	
			Issued 18 rounds 15 pr. shrapnel to 3rd Battery.	
	18/9/15		Supplied wagons + drew sand for 3rd Batt. Drew bricks at night. Supplied S.A.A. to 151st Bde. Issued 27 rounds ## to 2nd Batt., 44 rounds to 3rd Batt. 15 pr. Shrapnel. Drew bricks at night.	
	19/9/15		Supplied 44 rounds 3rd Batt., 57 rounds to 2nd Batt. 15 pr. Shrapnel	
			Supplied S.A.A. to 151st Bde. Drew bricks at night	
	20/9/15		Supplied 15 pr. Shrapnel 1st Batt. 216, 2nd Batt. 55, S.A.A. to 151st Bde.	
			Drew bricks at night.	
			LT ADAMSON returned from leave	
	21/9/15		Supplied 15 pr. Shrapnel 2nd Batt. 38, S.A.A. to 151st Bde.	
			Drew bricks at night. 12 men exchanged with batteries returned to their units & were replaced by other 12.	

WAR DIARY
or
INTELLIGENCE SUMMARY.

Army Form C. 2118

Place	Date	Hour	Summary of Events and Information	Remarks and references to Appendices
NIEPPE	22/9/15		Supplied 15 pr Shrapnel 1st Batt. 104, 2nd Batt. 50, SAA to 151st & 149th Bde. Sent 4 loads of bricks to complete 30,000.	CRO
	23/9/15		Supplied 15 pr Shrapnel 1st Batt. 30, 2nd Batt. 68, 3rd Batt. 44, SAA to 151 Bde.	CRO
	24/9/15		Supplied S.A.A. to 149th + 150th Bde, also 44 rounds 15 pr Shrapnel to 3rd Battery Res	CRO
		6 am	Received orders to be ready to move forward at 5.30 a.m. 25th.	
		7:30 am	Men attached to Batteries returned, battery reinforced to war.	
	25/9/15	2:15	Reveille	CRO
		5:30	Ready to move	
			Supplied 158 rounds to 1st Batt, 136 rounds to 2nd Batt, 132 rounds to 3rd Batt. 15 pr Shrapnel, SAA to 149th Bde	
	26/9/15	am	N.C.O. + 30 men proceeded to Armentières to buy 14 horses belonging to H.G.S.	CRO
		12.30	Supplied SAA to 149th Bde.	
		4.0	N.C.O. + 3 men returned	
	27/9/15	am	Burial party proceeded to Armentières, reported next day he's filling with water. H.Q. instructions to burn carcases. Party returned at 7 p.m. Supplied 110 rounds to 1st Battery. SAA to 149th + 150th Bde.	CRO
	28/9/15	8am	Burial party set off + returned at 6 p.m. jet being finished.	CRO

WAR DIARY
or
INTELLIGENCE SUMMARY

(Erase heading not required.)

Instructions regarding War Diaries and Intelligence Summaries are contained in F. S. Regs., Part II. and the Staff Manual respectively. Title pages will be prepared in manuscript.

Place	Date	Hour	Summary of Events and Information	Remarks and references to Appendices
NIEPPE.	28/9/15		Supplied S.A.A. to 149th Bde	CRC
	29/9/15		Supplied S.A.A. to 149th & 150th Bdes.	CRC
	30/9/15	6.30am	N.C.O. + 20 men proceeded to H.Q. of Ammunition to make dug outs. Returned 8 p.m.	CRC
			Supplied S.A.A. to 149th Bde	
		5.30 pm	Wagon proceeded to Houplines to cart timber from 2nd Batt. position to observing station.	

CRCommon Capt
O.C. Ammunition Column.
3rd North'd Bde R.F.A.

D/
7083

50th Division

2nd Northb'n Bde R.F.A. Ammn Coln

B VI
Sept 15

WAR DIARY
or
INTELLIGENCE SUMMARY.
(Erase heading not required.)

Army Form C. 2118.

Hour, Date, Place	Summary of Events and Information	Remarks and references to Appendices
1915.		
Sept. 1 NIEPPE	Routine. Regl. instructions to prepare for Wintering in Billets. Bde Major extracted particulars of requirements.	Present-Bertin
8. A.M.	2 Lt. Bonneville with Sgt. Priestley 1 orderly 6 Bandsmen + 12 Drivers + 1 S. Smith left with 6. G.S. wagons 24. Lt/b horses + limber awaits complete to G.H.Q. 4 Lorries to proceed to Boerzeele 2 days. 2 Lt. Bonneville in orderly to move back Staff Sgt. + Bandsmen to return by rail.— 4 Brick loading & unloading men Parties in good health.	Complete to G.H.Q. 4
4 P.M.	Lt. A.C. Mearsmann + Sanitary men Edward to BAILEUL & inspect Sanitary apparatus at Divisional HQ. Same in respect of filter straggles returned by train.	R.E.
" 2.	Routine. Brick loading & Salving. To BAILEUL for Coal — Regl. TV: a Bricks 36,000 — for house STANDINGS	
" 3	Routine. Heavy Rain. Pay.	

WAR DIARY
or
INTELLIGENCE SUMMARY.
(Erase heading not required.)

Army Form C. 2118.

Instructions regarding War Diaries and Intelligence Summaries are contained in F. S. Regs., Part II. and the Staff Manual respectively. Title pages will be prepared in manuscript.

Hour, Date, Place 1918	Summary of Events and Information	Remarks and references to Appendices
Sept. 4 NIEPPE	Routine	Coys & Trans Weather interferes with endure exercise somewhat with Brick Stampings & Wurters
Sept. 5 "	Routine	Crowder, Sand & Brick Fatigues
Sept. 6 "	Routine	Crowder Sand Fatigues for tram line Stradura supplying G.4 three hours. G/g R.E. Morris. Routine
Sept. 7 "	"	As above
Sept. 8 "	"	Watering continues @ Rue Lys to hide detstract with Train & G.S. Wagon as above.
Sept. 9 "	Routine	Leading Sand from Mr. Moir. 10 mile distant. Cryst Watson w/g 5 team. @ 7 PM reported left 1 hr burns G.S. Wagon in ditch off-front 5.3 a & x.6. Rot help B. Sinn 22.8.W. 6-8pm Sent-out-relief Party under S/Sgt Meahan Stering in Wagon @ 10.30 arrive Scene of accident drew limber & pack mules to fetch home remainder.

Army Form C. 2118.

WAR DIARY
or
INTELLIGENCE SUMMARY.
(Erase heading not required.)

Instructions regarding War Diaries and Intelligence Summaries are contained in F. S. Regs., Part II. and the Staff Manual respectively. Title pages will be prepared in manuscript.

Hour, Date, Place	Summary of Events and Information	Remarks and references to Appendices
Sept. 10 1915 NIEPPE 9.30 AM	2Lt Bonnewell Adjt from ARVILLE where he had lyr on 6 G.S. Wagons & Teams. Rtd with Sgt Kehun- leaving 12 horses with Vehicle & 4 Men	PAY
" 11 "	WATER continues very scarce. Watering 3 times a day at Rau Lys 12king 6 hrs day. Lieut S. G.S. Wagon to Bailleul for return.	
" 12 "	Church Parade. Working Party under 2.Lt. S. Williams ii / 16 men left @ 8.30 A.M. for forest NIEPPE, 15 MILES, to cut Fascines. for Road making.	
" 13 "	Water still scarce.	Fascines
" 14 "	Routine. S/Sgt Macnamara to H/Q act as Adjt in absence of Adjt on leave.	Fascines
" 15 "	Routine. Board held at Officers Billet. President Capt Wade upon lost G.S. harness Wagon Body. Sent Fatigue Party to forest Party.	PAY
" 16 "	Routine. 2.Lt Williams reported marching Fascines &c to Rlis of 80 per day.	Fascines

WAR DIARY
or
INTELLIGENCE SUMMARY.
(Erase heading not required.)

Army Form C. 2118.

Instructions regarding War Diaries and Intelligence Summaries are contained in F.S. Regs., Part II. and the Staff Manual respectively. Title pages will be prepared in manuscript.

Hour, Date, Place	Summary of Events and Information	Remarks and references to Appendices
Sept 17. NIEPPE	Routine. Brick laying, Cinder laying, Stations to	PAY
18 "	"	"
19 "	Church parade. Lieut. McEnnen ret'd from H.Q.	
20 "	Sgt. Stonehouse appointed Reng. Rdm to A.T.M. Army HQrs to Forest-Party brought back 30 Zerunn. Capt Smeeks left by 3.30 pm train from STERNWERK STATION on leave. Lt H.E. Macnamara on leave. E. Wagm hind to Poltuns n't d.	
21 "	Routine	
22 "	Routine. Fatigues as usual.	

Army Form C. 2118.

WAR DIARY
or
INTELLIGENCE SUMMARY.
(Erase heading not required.)

Instructions regarding War Diaries and Intelligence Summaries are contained in F. S. Regs., Part II. and the Staff Manual respectively. Title pages will be prepared in manuscript.

Hour, Date, Place	Summary of Events and Information	Remarks and references to Appendices
Sept 23	Routine preparing Camp for Winter. Belgians as previously.	
24	Routine. Recd. Standing Orders No 4. to be ready men 1st & 5.30 A.M. 2nd. PAY.	
25	Stand Bye. 2.30 AM. Wagon all ready. Horses up ready, harness in manuscript. Nothing -	
26	Church Parade. Captn/mules wi: Sim leave.	
27	10 Field Tent Khurinium Lamps dely A.S.C for men shelters. Water men Pluckique in Boot Farm. Men Horses in Farm.	
28	Routine. Belgians as before.	

Forms/C. 2118/10

Army Form C. 2118.

WAR DIARY
or
INTELLIGENCE SUMMARY.
(Erase heading not required.)

Instructions regarding War Diaries and Intelligence Summaries are contained in F.S. Regs., Part II. and the Staff Manual respectively. Title pages will be prepared in manuscript.

Hour, Date, Place	Summary of Events and Information	Remarks and references to Appendices
Sept 29	Routine. Lt. L. Williams & Foren Pati, N.4 Jun FOREST NIEPPE reported down with Men. 1200 F Reims & 4½ Coys + 2 men in Charge. Prior Ayr En duty to Ex.	
" 30	Routine. South of Trayen Road - Guns maintaining in A1 Condition. Water maintaining Scarce during the Month. 1 Sect. of Brigade reconnoitred Horse Standing completed down to Mult & half new Jervis Road way 15 Stm Line + Park Complete.	

Summary of Ammunition Issued during the Month.

Shell. 2004 Rds of 80 Tage
         677   "   9 Old ..
       ———
       2681

SAA 214,000 Rds.

P.H.A. 196. Rds.
West Stringis 50 Rds.

H. W. Sanders
Comm'g. 2nd N'brian Amm Col.
Capt. R.F.A. (T)

Form/C. 2118

Confidential

WAR DIARY

VOL VII

1/9/15 to 30/9/15

2 New Am. Col.

50th Division

12/7437

50th Div. Ammn. Col

Sep - Dec '15

Vol III

Confidential

War Diary
of
Lieut Colonel F. W. Cluff
50th Divisional Ammunition Column
from 1st Sept. 1915 to 31st Oct. 1915
Volume I

WAR DIARY or INTELLIGENCE SUMMARY

Army Form C. 2118.

Place	Date	Hour	Summary of Events and Information	Remarks and references to Appendices
NIEPPE	3/9/15 to 3/10/15		Reviewed the whole of September in the same place with the exception of a very satisfactory increase in the supply of Hand Grenades. There is nothing to report beyond the ordinary routine work.	
NIEPPE	1/10/15, 23/10/15, 24/10/15		Battery of inspectors to found. Moved Headquarters and one section to the area occupied by 1st and 4th Sections. Have come to O.C. advanced section of the 21st Divisional Ammunition Column, who took over control of Ammunition Trench Stones & the following Grenades. 660. Cel. supply and also the following: 9/15b. No 5 (Mills). 6/15b. Ball. 2,000 Verey Pigeon 280. No 3. (Rifle) 9/15b. No 5 (Mills) 6/15b. No 11. 1½" Illuminating 504. 1½" Illuminating and the following Rifts. 24/12. 1½". Illuminating and 85 Rockets. with Parachute. 130 1" Illuminating.	
	26/10/15		Moved into new area 2½ miles north of HAZEBROUCK.	

121/7439

50th Division

2nd Northumbrian Bde RFA Ammn Coln

Vol VIII

Oct 15

Army Form C. 2118.

WAR DIARY
or
INTELLIGENCE SUMMARY.
(Erase heading not required.)

Instructions regarding War Diaries and Intelligence Summaries are contained in F.S. Regs., Part II. and the Staff Manual respectively. Title pages will be prepared in manuscript.

Hour, Date, Place		Summary of Events and Information	Remarks and references to Appendices
Gt NIEPPE	Oct. 1. 1915.	Routine	Daily Fatigues making Brick Standings + laying chain Road leading Rubber teshn. chain cutting 4. PAY
	" 2		1.9.S. Wagon Sent-R.2. park broke rear iron axle - disclosing (a latent-defect)
	" 3		Fatigue work in Lines + On entrance gate way 4.
	" 4		Renewed Brandine iron from no 4 Sect. Lewis M.G. 1.9.S. Wagon axle fractured. 6dr Gun in manufacture. Reports to O.A.D.9.S.
	" 5		Sent 1.9.S. wagon with broken axle to " Corp Workshop BAILLEUL making Bridge tread el main entrance to Am. Park Recd 80 cisterns from Bargue El Canal
	" 6		Fatigues Recd a new 1.9.S. Wagon sent to 2 Corp Workshop @ Bailleul has been forwarded to-or. - Rue qu Zarcin from Bargue

Army Form C. 2118.

WAR DIARY
or
INTELLIGENCE SUMMARY.
(Erase heading not required.)

Instructions regarding War Diaries and Intelligence Summaries are contained in F.S. Regs., Part II. and the Staff Manual respectively. Title pages will be prepared in manuscript.

Hour, Date, Place		Summary of Events and Information	Remarks and references to Appendices
DIEPPE	Oct. 7 1915	Routine	Recd. alarm for attack in of Hospital Hulk Bitter.
"	8	"	Midnight Wagon transport 150° with 54th. Pay
"	9	"	Helium as usual
"	10	"	Musketry on Wagons attached & re marched 10" blue Circle with No 11 in centre.
"	11	Sunday. Church parade	
"	12	Routine	Midnight orders rec'd to cease Supplying 150° & Mds with 54th
"	13	"	G.S.E. maneuvres went in trams. Recd. from 2 Corps Workshops 1. G.S. Wagon repaired in lieu of one. Midnight order rec'd Cease Supplying 5A th L 150/9/12 etc Sent Bare Office letters to Base for storage.
"	14	Orders for State of Special Vigilance recd. & come into force at dawn. Reveille 4.30 A.M. teams harnessed up at 5 A.M.	
"	"	State of Special Vigilance Reveille 4.30. teams harnessed up at 5 A.M.	

Army Form C. 2118.

WAR DIARY
or
INTELLIGENCE SUMMARY.
(Erase heading not required.)

Instructions regarding War Diaries and Intelligence Summaries are contained in F.S. Regs., Part II. and the Staff Manual respectively. Title pages will be prepared in manuscript.

Hour, Date, Place		Summary of Events and Information	Remarks and references to Appendices
NIEPPE	Dec. 15th 1915	Routine. 2Lt. W.T.O. Bennett, to J Battery to instruction. Returned matter of Sentries by Court Martial on Dr. Gunn Hogue being in suspense for review by C.R.A. Pay.	on T.O.O. in Trenches. Hogue to R.a. Office
"	16	" Talgun tr.	
"	17	Sunday. A.M. Mr. H.E. McNamara rej[oined] from leave. P.M. 2 Lt. L.R. Williams Gunners on leave	From Sgt. Webster Shoe maker allowed sent to Hospital
"	18	Routine. 2Lt. Bennett to J Battery to return as F.O.O. 1 O.R. Wy. sent with rations to forward party & to bring been Willis for road making	Re. Allied' Material for Guides Wood hut. (?)
"	19	Routine. Talgun tr.	
"	20	Routine. 9.0 A.M. Lt. Bennett rej. from 4th Hy. Tour of duty a F.O.O. C.R.A. advised through 108 Office Sentries in Dr. Payne Hogue had not been recommended for remission.	
"	21	Routine. Completed Brick Standing Bridge into Park & foundation for Gathering Am. Waggon	

WAR DIARY
or
INTELLIGENCE SUMMARY.
(Erase heading not required.)

Army Form C. 2118.

Place	Hour, Date	Summary of Events and Information	Remarks and references to Appendices
NIEPPE	Feb. 22. 6/15	Routine. Instructed to supply 149 In Bde with S.A.A. from 8 A.M. until A.E.d. of 94 Bde A.E.r ready supply from 6 A.M. ordered to resupply, all 15½ A.M. regn for 15/6 guns remaining in action until midnight 23rd. Get for 15/6	6 A.M. 2d Rammers arrive 7.0.0. Rec'd 2 Mb drawn from Middle Vet Sect
	" 23	Routine. Rec'd orders to prepare for a move to a Rest Camp. & to prepare accommodation for men & horses. 1 L. Sect. M.R. Battery & single gun & teams from 1 in Yr Battery 6 P.M. Lt Rammers on to duty. Cleaning up horses, grooming, wagon detail as above began to arrive.	
		6.30 P.M. 2 Lt Sir Williams arr. 4 A.M. from France.	
	" 24	Ammder. Brenda Camp finished at 9.0 A.M. in following order Commences - 2 Lt J.H.WRIGHT ATTACHED. POSTED C. Am. Ca. AVC. 2 h Am - ed. complete with 2 extn G. Wagon & Mr Am Ca left Sect of N.R. Battery. Guns fun & detail of 1st 2 2 R. Battery. at 11-5 A.M. Passed through BAILLEUL. Halted for 1 hr between Ferd & Point between BAILLEUL & METEREN – e 11.30 A.M. moved off at 1.0 P.M. through FLETRE ot 1.30 P.M. Halted for 10 minutes between FLETRE & CAESTRE c 2.10 P.M.	
CAESTRE.		Arrived at CAESTRE @ 1-30- P.M. Reached Billets for Am. Ca et 3.30. P.M. et fain [W.] V.6. C./ × 1 Sheet 27 Passed Vehicles tot up Lines - 4.0. P.M. Rain fell.	

WAR DIARY
or
INTELLIGENCE SUMMARY.
(Erase heading not required.)

Army Form C. 2118.

Instructions regarding War Diaries and Intelligence Summaries are contained in F.S. Regs., Part II. and the Staff Manual respectively. Title pages will be prepared in manuscript.

Hour, Date, Place			Summary of Events and Information	Remarks and references to Appendices
CAESTRE	Oct.	25	Routine. Completing store lines Sanitary Telephone &c after details left behind. 10.30 A.M. Sent 2 G.S. wagons to NIEPPE to collect men brought to left behind.	Rain.
"	"	26	Routine. 11 A.M. Col. M. Stundall visited Kinspelier Camp. No issue of Staff. 1 Case of Mess Wine. Hoisted notice all leave withdrawn until orders ascertained. 2 G.S. wagon ats from NIEPPE.	Have been a bus full no provision made for their stationing. Rain.
"	"	27	Routine. 11.0 A.M. Sent 5 G.S. wagon to FOREST NIEPPE for firewood. 11.30. Sgt. A. BRAIM sent to Base to demobilize. 4.30 P.M. Lined up Road to cheer H.M. KING GEORGE V who passed in motor car.	Rain.
"	"	28	Routine. Some men of home S&C by endeavour.	Rain.
"	"	29	Routine. 11.0 A.M. 1 G.S. Wagon sent to First Hotspur - 2 P.R. Pulling prss. 10 A.M. Sent 8 G.S. wagon to Forest Nieppe for firewood. 4 P.M. Sheep Skin Waircoats issued from Ordnance.	Rain.
"	"	30	Routine. Unloaded all ammunition & checked same.	Rain.
"	"	31	Routine. Sunday. Church parade. Summary men.	Rain.

WAR DIARY
or
INTELLIGENCE SUMMARY.
(Erase heading not required.)

Army Form C. 2118.

Hour, Date, Place	Summary of Events and Information	Remarks and references to Appendices
	The health of the men throughout the month has been excellent - at least - over a week every man has had a hot bath + great care paid to boots. The horses continue in A.1. condition. Careful attention being paid to disinfecting brushes + harness. Skin trouble entirely avoided. Salt- (Rock) + Chops daily added to feeds - All horses re-branded + taken re-numbered during the month All re-shod - the month. The following Ammunition reserve during the month. 368 Rounds S.A. 15 pr. Gun. 20 fuze Ann. 233,000 " " S.A.A. Mk VII 403 Bomb Grenades. The horse lines at MIEPPE were entirely constructed in Brick. Standing Roads + Entrance Bridge built + ground spaces with water lashes for parking the Am. wagons - 7 wooden sheds for the men erected	Standrake Capt 11724 of 2 MRCd.

50th Div. Amm. Col.

Nov. 1

Vol IV

121 / 7655

WAR DIARY
or
INTELLIGENCE SUMMARY
(Erase heading not required.)

Army Form C. 2118.

Hour, Date, Place	Summary of Events and Information	Remarks and references to Appendices
Nov 1st	Very wet weather. Horses standing very dead.	
2nd	Supply of drinks coming in very slowly.	
3rd	Nothing to report.	
4th	All horses now in shocking condition. 3rd NORTH: Brigade being the worst near ROOTE-BOOM.	
5th	Nothing to report.	
6th		
7th	CRA returned from leave of absence to ENGLAND	
8th	CRA started inspection of the subsection per bipock in marching order in lines.	
9th	D.A. began to move to new area EAST of CAESTRE – HAZEBROUCK railway.	
10th	Above were completed.	
11th	Completion of the exchange of horses for mules. DAC receiving mules from Indian Cav, 61 Btty. Resg Cof R.F.A. Horses of the horses had five

WAR DIARY
or
INTELLIGENCE SUMMARY

(Erase heading not required.)

Army Form C. 2118.

Hour, Date, Place	Summary of Events and Information	Remarks and references to Appendices
12	Camp owing to bad conditions.	
13th	Pathing to report. Ditto	
14th	G.O.C. 50th Division and FRA inspected the Horse & D.A.C.	
15th		
16th	Returned wet weather.	
17th	Nothing to report. Bricks for stables & lining wing delayed.	
18	Major Thomson Brigade Major proceeded on leave of absence. Captain F.G. MYERS assumed duties of B.M. Captain C.N. BRIMS 15th Div. Arty. & Staff Captain.	
19th	Material for horse lines, shelters and cook houses arriving in bulk.	

Army Form C. 2118.

WAR DIARY
or
INTELLIGENCE SUMMARY
(Erase heading not required.)

Instructions regarding War Diaries and Intelligence Summaries are contained in F.S. Regs., Part II. and the Staff Manual respectively. Title pages will be prepared in manuscript.

Hour, Date, Place	Summary of Events and Information	Remarks and references to Appendices
20th	Brigade completing their shelters and huts for the men. Nothing to report.	
21st		
22nd	Brigade leaving one hour to go for ammunition to D.A.C. in preparation for store change to 18 pr equipment.	
23rd	A brigade's ateel of 18 pr guns and respective equipment received in 15 pr equipment retained & store hrs HOUTBROUCK Station.	
24th	Remainder of 18 M equipment & complete 50 JH received.	
25th	Bdy cdr view their 18 pr ammunition horse drawn on CAESTRE.	

WAR DIARY
or
INTELLIGENCE SUMMARY
(Erase heading not required.)

Army Form C. 2118.

Hour, Date, Place	Summary of Events and Information	Remarks and references to Appendices
25	Saw Div. and rather severe frost.	
26	Cold and wet.	
27	Very severe frost indeed.	
28	Rathawed wet and soft in places. Horselines very bad conditions indeed.	
29	Very wet and cold	
30	Very fine day. G.O.C Second ARMY inspected the artillery of 50th Division. The D.A wanted past the ARMY COMMANDER at a point on the STRAZEELE - MOOLENACKER road. The inspection proved satisfactory. Taking 47 minutes. The ARMY COMMANDER afterwards started the 23rd & 31st trench mortars at BORRE.	

1/2" Nonitubulan Annin. Col.

Nov. 1

vol VIII

121/7655

50 k/Twain

Army Form C. 2118.

WAR DIARY
or
INTELLIGENCE SUMMARY.
(Erase heading not required.)

Instructions regarding War Diaries and Intelligence Summaries are contained in F. S. Regs., Part II. and the Staff Manual respectively. Title pages will be prepared in manuscript.

Hour, Date, Place		Summary of Events and Information	Remarks and references to Appendices
FARM 3000 S.W. of CAESTRE Map Ref. W.2.B. 9x7. Ref Sheet: 27.1/40 – Nov. 1	You Monday.	Routine. Special Riding + Driving drill Classes AM Gun drill in Afternoon.	Rain.
do	" 2	2/Lt Wright A.V.C. reported in Bttn orders as attached to Am Col from 24.10.15. Special training Driving drill Gun drill	Rain
do	" 3	Routine. Special training Driving drill & gun drill training Foreman Gun Court hippo.	drying Ammunition Rain When possible
do	" 4	Routine. Special training Driving drill Gun drill	Rain
do	" 5	Routine. Special Classes as above. training foreman from Fred hippo.	Rain PAY
do	" 6	Routine Special Classes as above.	Rain.

WAR DIARY
or
INTELLIGENCE SUMMARY.
(Erase heading not required.)

Army Form C. 2118.

Hour, Date, Place	Summary of Events and Information	Remarks and references to Appendices
Farm S.W. of CAESTRE Map Ref Sheet 27 1/40000 Nov 7 W.0.6.9x7	Sunday. Ch. Parade.	
" 8	Routine. General Camp Fatigues filling in holes in horse lines & clearing Camp to prepare for moving out.	Rain.
Farm @ BORRE E.1.b.6x7 Ref Map Sheet 36A. " 9	at 2.P.M. Struck Camp & proceeded through BORRE to a Farm 1000 yds S. of BORRE. with R+L Sections. Major Ref E.1.b.6x7. Sheet 16A arrived at 2.45.P.M. Put up horse lines new Picketts. Reported to BOS 4/4 at W.20.C.2.2x8.	
" 10	1. G.S. wagon to draw Forage. Telephone laid to Hdqtrs of W.20.C. 6x7 Ref Sheet 27. Return of Wdiv. accommodation rendered to Hdqtrs 4/4.	
" 11	10.G.S. Wagons to Mr. des CATS on Bde Baned Fatigue. 2 G.S. " " " " in Forage Fatigue. Re 2 Guns from N.R. Nillery for dull purposes sent to remain until further order.	
" 12	12. G.S. Wagons to Mr des CATS on Bde Baned Fatigue. Fatigue to CAESTRE to draw medicine & rations, shelter. Spare Gun Drill	
" 13	10.G.S. Wagon to Mr des CATS on Bde Baned Fatigue. 2 G.S. " " " " to Forage Fatigue. Re'd 2. 15 pr Guns from 2.R. Battery for training Gunners.	PAY

Army Form C. 2118.

WAR DIARY
or
INTELLIGENCE SUMMARY.
(Erase heading not required.)

Instructions regarding War Diaries and Intelligence Summaries are contained in F.S. Regs., Part II. and the Staff Manual respectively. Title pages will be prepared in manuscript.

Hour, Date, Place	Summary of Events and Information	Remarks and references to Appendices
BORRE.		
Nov. 14	Sunday. K.Coy 9th Fusiliers made a voluntary statement re stolen car of News Views in night oct 24=. Ch. Panier	
" 15	Recur. Q-stewards from men indicated in stolen van. Building harness stables preparing Winter Shoeing. Rouin~ Spare Gun drill	
" 16	Rec'd 16 Re inforcements all guns in except 2. Simulated 50% defective M.Wirn in B½ Sans Fatigue. 8. Q.S Wagon to M.Wirn in B½ Sans Fatigue. 2.G.S " " Various increased resources to O.C. 18 W in Coe	From England. 2 Lt. R.M. NICKELS reported for duty (Attached Officer)
" 17	Lt. Moss Blundell taking Am Col parunrs in Stn when Coe Spare Gun drill " "	
" 18	10. G.S Wagons to M. NOIR for B½ Sans Fatigues. 3 " Moss Blundell taking Am Col from Anforges Gun drill. Routines.	
" 19	Lt. Moss Blundell does M. Change against of Kuln M Bentley & Cpl Moors. All Gunnery Repairments Gun drill	

Army Form C. 2118.

WAR DIARY
or
INTELLIGENCE SUMMARY.
(Erase heading not required.)

Instructions regarding War Diaries and Intelligence Summaries are contained in F.S.Regs., Part II and the Staff Manual respectively. Title pages will be prepared in manuscript.

Hour, Date, Place	Summary of Events and Information	Remarks and references to Appendices
FARM at point E.1.6.6x7 SHEET 36A	Sgt Bradley & two Gunners to N.R. Battery for instruction.	
Nov 20	8am Alt & one suspended 2.5" Def. resumed this day. 10 G.S. Wagons to Mt. NOIR for Sand Filter for 13/de.	PAY
" 21	Sunday. Ch. parade. 2 G.S. Wagons sent to Brickyard at Hazebrouck for Bricks for Beds.	
" 22	Sent. Dr. FLETCHER to attend a Bugger & Signalling class at Depot at MERRIS. MAILE fuze enemy in the heavy A/c.	
" 23	Arrived at HAZEBROUCK STATION of 12 new 18/pr guns also 12 new 18 pr Am. Wagons. The letter reached AM Col. Lines @ 6.30 pm. Sent to Rail-head. All 15 pr gun Spares - sent to Army S/c. MAILE fuze enemy in the heavy A/c.	The 6 G.S. Wagons & their eight horses for 15pr equipment remain with A/c.
" 24	Right Sect of Am.Col. arrived B64 Rds 15pr Gun Am at Rail-head STRAZEELE	
" 25	10 G.S.wagons to Mt. Noir Loading Sand for Battery Horse lines. 12 new Limbed Am.Wagons & CAIESTRE to load 912 Rds 18 pr gun ammunition - Part new Store for Ice.wagons received Bdy S/c. 3 H.b. drivers with estic - 1 mule & 1 severe case of Horse Fold (No 2708 died) Officers instruction in 18 pr Gun at "I" Battery	

WAR DIARY
or
INTELLIGENCE SUMMARY.
(Erase heading not required.)

Army Form C. 2118.

Instructions regarding War Diaries and Intelligence Summaries are contained in F. S. Regs., Part II. and the Staff Manual respectively. Title pages will be prepared in manuscript.

Hour, Date, Place	Summary of Events and Information	Remarks and references to Appendices
BORRE hour 26 Farm at point E.1.b. 6x7. Sheet 96.A	2.9.t wagon in Bwsh Fatigue. Gun instruction in new 18 pr guns at 1st Battery. 10.0 noon alarm died have found rattling in Shrawl nap? midyets mage. through H.E. in detonator. Report in MAIZE Forge Inspection send to 2/9.	FROST.
" 27	5 gun Court Martial held of Am Col Pellet— 10.0 AM. Comd: Pandel Major 7.9 b Yorkestone 1 Hb var 12th Member 3 Copts. I. Washam 50 lamb Rd 4. T. Wade 2 htm 124-12th Prison Copl. Ryer & Gr. Peck. 10.9's wagon to Mt. Noir men- friends. I. His own Colic at night.	FROST PAY
" 28	Sunday. Bathque thynamin Cleaning Conference at 120 30/2. Indenting for new Stores.	FROST.
" 29	Fatigues Hyseurum Cleaning. Pole keepers all day.—	THAW. Rain
" 30	Inspection by the Army Commander. First Parade / press 18pr. am wagon team. Parade of my heavy through mud. 18 R. in increments arrived. A. B.H.C.A.	Fine.

WAR DIARY or INTELLIGENCE SUMMARY.

Army Form C. 2118.

(Erase heading not required.)

Instructions regarding War Diaries and Intelligence Summaries are contained in F.S. Regs., Part II. and the Staff Manual respectively. Title pages will be prepared in manuscript.

Hour, Date, Place	Summary of Events and Information	Remarks and references to Appendices
Summary.	The first half of the month was very wet — raining continuously for 11 days. Having no facilities at the farm for drying the men's equipment-rifles for 7 days.	
Rest Camp	after 3 days the 18 pdr carts allowed became water-logged & 1 1/2 inch R.B.L. guns ran practically into the ruts full of mud. Since the rains were in part of the time 12" deep in slush.	was not the result.
	It was impossible to dispense with winter a Consider Luther boots in much superior to Mackintosh Capes & both are much superior to Mackintosh Cape Gum. boots were used in	Lung Col Shaw Cox — very much the same Carl Kazamis Carl.
Ammunition fired during the month	Despite the heavy rain special Grenade & Rev. Drill instruction to Trench Routine — Tactical was carried on throughout the area with the R.E.U. moved into	BORRIE area on the 9 hour. He gave key dining
15 pr. Gun = 15 Rds 303 SAA = 11,000 " To Rail Heads = 864 Rds 18 pr =	The Bove in Tatum area. The site of the A.C.S. Vehicles away Sand Saligur South hi-hour thr-	10 miles away. des Col J.
	The Bournes brought Gen. Sir 19 & 20 hrs. equal to 6 hrs daily for hour Major was received from the Dinner in the Cov. died.	It is the C.O. died. Danes
	were at the Casm ', me a Black man at least at the P. Mule. in the Indjulai orange was formed in Ait Dimeele	ten the 23 hour

Capt. R. A. Shah
Capt. 9/2th A.S.A.

CONFIDENTIAL

WAR DIARY. TRAIN RAW

2nd Am. Col. SHAMMUS DETACHMENT

Vol. IX
From 1.11.15
To 30.11.15

(56th)
2/North" Amum Col.

Dec
Vol. IX

121/7957

WAR DIARY
or
INTELLIGENCE SUMMARY.
(Erase heading not required.)

Army Form C. 2118.

Hour, Date, Place	Summary of Events and Information	Remarks and references to Appendices
BORRE Dec 1. Wed 9 1915	Routine L& Jegers	
" 2	Rifle Inspection –	
" 3	9 men transferred to N.R. Battery 2 dr. W.W. Whyte Stevens to Am. Col. gun N.R. Battery 2/Lr Williams of the Am. Col. attached to N.R. Battery	
" 3	1 Gunner + 1 S/Smith transferred to N.R. Battery from AC1. 6. G.S. wagons mk X * handed over to O/C 2 Sect. to A.C.1.	
" 4	14 N.C.O.'s & men rec'd reinforcements posts to Am. Col.	
" 5 Sun	Routine	
" 6	3/4 + Batterman proceeded to Training Camp at WATTEN all vacated Billets & Grains left in charge O/C Am Col. (Re. 19 Sick Horses (mostly very temporary Admrd. Gun Battern.) W.K.C. machine gun H W.T.O. Penn well attd to 2 BR. Battn.	

WAR DIARY
or
INTELLIGENCE SUMMARY.
(Erase heading not required.)

Army Form C. 2118.

Hour, Date, Place	Summary of Events and Information	Remarks and references to Appendices
BORRE Dec. 7	Routine. Inspection Meeting up all Battery Stores.	
" Dec. 8	Coy. R.E. took possession of 1 + 3 Battery Farm Billets.	
	Routine. Brush fatigue. Vailled N.b.A. + Billeting Guards at Battery & received. Watch from Hospitals & leave to WATTEN.	
" Dec. 9	Inspection of all vacated Battery Billets. Tools School Inspection.	
" Dec. 10	Capt. Smallen rode to VOLKERINCKOVE to report in Training @ 2 hour H/Q.	
" Dec. 11	Bury left with Am.Col. men to training Camp. H.H.S. Macnamara in Charge of 15.C.M. All horses exercised from Lines in Farm Juls & Road — when here Lines set up.	
" Dec. 12	Harness Inspection. Routine Fatigues.	

Army Form C. 2118.

WAR DIARY
or
INTELLIGENCE SUMMARY.
(Erase heading not required.)

Instructions regarding War Diaries and Intelligence Summaries are contained in F.S. Regs., Part II. and the Staff Manual respectively. Title pages will be prepared in manuscript.

Hour, Date, Place	Summary of Events and Information	Remarks and references to Appendices
BORRE. 1916. 13	364/b Horses arrived from Am. Col. bro	
" 14	Routine Fatigues. Rout in Inspection of Vehicles.	
" 15	Routine. Checking Ammunition	
" 16	Capt. Kimsler ret'd from VOLKERINGHOVE to take over command of Am. Col.	
" 17	2 him. Does 1/10 + 3 Batteries up" from Training two Veterinary Insp.	
" 18	Schwz. 888 Rounds 18lb. Gun Am to 50 Bg F.Ch. Returned. All hrn attached from Col. back to Batteries also ret'g all Battery Sick horses left at A.Col. awaiting Bde Training — 16 out of 19 sick horses being returned cured.

(73989) W.4141—463. 400,000. 9/14. H.&J.Ltd. Forms/C. 2118/10.

WAR DIARY
or
INTELLIGENCE SUMMARY.
(Erase heading not required.)

Army Form C. 2118.

Hour, Date, Place	Summary of Events and Information	Remarks and references to Appendices
BORRE Oct. 19	Sunday. Left Billets at BORRE @ 8.30 A.M. 9.30 am @ CAISTRE turned (east) order of R.Major. 1.30 P.M. left BORRE Billets again & arrived - 2.30 am Boeschepe 5.10 am Westoutre @ 6.0 P.M. all Bde Am. Cols. on move. in new Billet - 8.15 P.M. with R.F.A. Section 1 2 & 3 no am. Cols. Billets	ATTACK on YPRES am Godewaersvelde @ 4.40 9.15 P.M. - Pte Fretaction 9.4 amp sent to hospital
RENINGHELST " 20	Reported to Battle Insurance for instructions re supply of ammunition. Battalion ad-functions probable. Belty W. Gunn & Infantin. T. Officers W. Linn	men Billets in Barns
RENINGHELST " 21 G. 22. d. 1 x 4 Sheet 28	Issued S.A.A. R.150 " Inf Bde. also Verey Lights.	also in 2 Lany Huts
" 21	Telephone in Barn Speaking up Church.	no Gun ammunit.
" 22	Sent M. ordulies round all Inf Bde W.L. in Turn. Issued S.A.A.	quarter for R.F.A
" 23	Posted M. ordely with T. Officer 145 Inf Bde Issued S.A.H.	
" 24	Capt Anyon o/c A.R.H. Lt Kirkbyshe solo W/u Vinden Am. Park. 2 lb. Whyte ordered to report c/AFW attached 122 Battery W. Lin	

WAR DIARY
or
INTELLIGENCE SUMMARY.
(Erase heading not required.)

Army Form C. 2118.

Instructions regarding War Diaries and Intelligence Summaries are contained in F.S. Regs., Part II and the Staff Manual respectively. Title pages will be prepared in manuscript.

Hour, Date, Place		Summary of Events and Information	Remarks and references to Appendices
1915			
RENINGHELST Farm West 25 G.22.d.1x4	Rurkine.	Xmas dinner at 1-0 pm Belgian Interpreter to 5o biv Artillery reported to Am. Col Mess Mr G. TANNING - B. Officer Belgian Mission	MENU. Roast Beef Veg't. Plum Pudding 2 Bottles Beer Nuts & Crackers
" 26		Visited the A/a & Dde of KRUISTAAT. Returned Baggage Wagon with W. Teasdale Atma ho 22 to A.C. 2 U. W.T.O. Communic. orders to R. Jones & Acton & Gunnery BERTHEN	
" 27		Gen Wilkinson K.S.H. visited the Lines. Received S. Rds. ammunition. Checked same numerics. Withdrew bridelim from 1 & 3 Batty W Lines	
" 28		Bo Coupland detailed R.S.M. orderly at H/Q	Transport
" 29		9 drivers & 17 horses attd to 149 Inf Bde T. Officer 2/L Bonnewell reported sent to mr noirs Rest Station from School of Gunnery - BERTHEN	
" 30		Below 3. G.S. Wagon loads of Ammedon to 149 Inf Bde " 72 Rounds of Shrapnel to M Riding Battery as keeping Gun Class practicing loading & fuze setting Sent - 6 men to N.R. Battery gun positions.	Alt. Vet. Officer left to report for duty at Mobile Vet. Sect. Instructed to fill up Sundries Wagon 888 Rounds (24 Inches)

(73989) W4141-463. 400,000. 9/14. H.&J.Ltd. Forms/C. 2118/10.

WAR DIARY
or
INTELLIGENCE SUMMARY.

Army Form C. 2118.

Hour, Date, Place	Summary of Events and Information	Remarks and references to Appendices
PENINGHELST 9.22.d.1x4 Sheet 28 1915 Dec 31	Routine Reported of C.R.A. rec'd instructions re reserve of SAA & Grenades - forming camp - Erecting Spare gun stores. Am. Col. orderly at/g KRUISTRAAT ADV. Completed to dispatch shell - in bank shrapnel Worms rec'd 7 p.m. 30/12/15.— Summary of Ammunition supplied during the month. During the month, painted trips all vehicles. As many men as possible attended Bde. Training Camp. Moved up Gun Res- & forward section S. YPRES. Vehicles employed in Engineer & Infantry Transport Officer. Ypres - Roads in many places only gun - passable; daily broken wheels + broken field stores.	3 Tons of Ammunition arriving for 1/6 Home France shortly in exchange for our H.B. During the month gun 18-DY QF = 256 Rounds NOTE Siege Battalion went into action they have been supplied to ammo 9/6 sw. + since by Motored direct to Wagon lines — SAA 129.000 Rounds Grenades 6.064 [signature] Capt. R.F.A. (T) Comdg. 2nd NH MIDLAND Amm. Col.

Confidential
War Diary
of
Lieut Colonel J. W. Cluff
50th Divisional Ammunition Column
from 1/12/15 to 31/12/15
Volume IV

Army Form C. 2118.

WAR DIARY
or
INTELLIGENCE SUMMARY.
(Erase heading not required.)

Instructions regarding War Diaries and Intelligence Summaries are contained in F. S. Regs., Part II. and the Staff Manual respectively. Title pages will be prepared in manuscript.

Place	Date	Hour	Summary of Events and Information	Remarks and references to Appendices
BORRE	1/17/15		Handed over to the Indian Division 101 mules in exchange for L.D. horses	
	3/17/15		Handed over to the Indian Division 162 mules in exchange for L.D. horses. Wrote to R.A. section 3rd echelon for reinforcements to complete to new establishment, urgently required.	
	5/17/15		Received from Brigade Ammunition Column 16 G.S. wagons which they held surplus on being supplied with limbered wagons for gun ammunition. Indented for 6 G.S. wagons (complete harness) to complete to establishment.	
	6/17/15 to 21/17/15		Nothing of importance to record	

1577 Wt. W10791/1773 500,000 1/15 D. D. & L. A.D.S.S./Forms/C. 2118.

Army Form C. 2118.

WAR DIARY
or
INTELLIGENCE SUMMARY.
(Erase heading not required.)

Place	Date	Hour	Summary of Events and Information	Remarks and references to Appendices
BRRE	22/1/15		Moved to a position 2½ miles S.W. of POPERINGHE and took over from 9th Divisional Ammunition Column found both the ground and the huts in a disgracefully dirty and insanitary condition reported to Divisional Headquarters to this effect. The situation of Horse Standings in two of the sections had been badly chosen no consideration having been given to winter conditions, in one instance the standings of 3 that of the 2nd section had to be abandoned as the approach to it was practically flooded by the stream running between it and the field by which it had to be approached.	
	23/1/15 to 31/1/15		Nothing of importance to report, with the exception that the reinforcements asked for on the 31st Dec have not yet arrived.	J.G. Swift Lieut Colonel 50th Divisional Ammunition Column

1/2 N'thumian Anmd Cnl.
—————
Jan
—————
Vol XI
x

55

Army Form C. 2118.

WAR DIARY
or
INTELLIGENCE SUMMARY.
(Erase heading not required.)

Hour, Date, Place	Summary of Events and Information	Remarks and references to Appendices
RENINGHELST FARM. Jany 1 1916 G.22.d.1×4	Brownin Spare Gun Stores & Allwin Primus &c	
" 2	Applied to O.C. for instruction re issue of Gun Stores	
" 3 Sunday		
" 4	Sent in a complaint to A.S.C. rep. supply of forage.	
" 5	Collected 222 Rounds of 18 pr Gun Amn from W. Lim supplied 1 2 I.R. By with lower pumps. Sgt. Newby transferred from R.S. to N.V.R. Battery.	
" 6	Mule Odr. re animality distributed. 13 Sub-sect 14 Pet Male Re-pointed out making upon all Vehicles. Lt. Gryson H.L. Ogden reported @ 7.30:- Obtained from R.E. back S. Wood Bridge to improve approaches. First issue of Gun Ammunition. 2 Officers attached for instruction posted in W.O.2 81/4.	B & Complains died of Wounds No 17 C.C.S. Poperinghe.

Army Form C. 2118.

WAR DIARY
or
INTELLIGENCE SUMMARY.
(Erase heading not required.)

Hour, Date, Place	Summary of Events and Information	Remarks and references to Appendices
RENINGHELST 1916.		
G.22.d.1×4 JANY. 7.	Complained to A.S.C. re Forage Supply. B/of supply empty from Tues to F.R. for maxim limber. Indented for 2 wood bridges arrived for fire-pack. 2nd Lt Bonnewell left to train Reststation for BH&S.	
" 8	2nd Lt W.W. Whyte ret'd to R.E.A. for duty. Procured hip baths for maxim hussars. Bircles W/SE to Falken & Lt Campbell re his own duties to Campbell reported from Ecole Shavine course –	PAY
" 9	Sunday. Sent 5 horse men to N.K. Battery to dig.	
" 10	Cayteneen & BAILEUL – dentist.	
" 11	Phone connection made with Wey[...] [...] of Nottawa H&Q. 2nd Lt W.W. Whyte left in ambulance for Mars. R.E. Officer collecting information as hutting – Rec'd Wigan for A.T.C –	
" 12	Lt. L.K. Williams N.O. to A.C. for duty Rep'd US Lut-Horsen unavailable against Snyder. Tel censorships sent in to Rec'd H.Q.— Steam dolphinel. 2 large Aerial Bombs in neighbouring field.	Ann hy 260 dies Rec'd Ku Censor Stamp.

WAR DIARY
or
INTELLIGENCE SUMMARY.
(Erase heading not required.)

Army Form C. 2118.

Hour, Date, Place	Summary of Events and Information	Remarks and references to Appendices
RENNINGHELST 1916		
G.22.d.1x4 JANY. 13	No 8&9 2/b. with 149 Inf. Bde. dined Lock Laur. No 872 s/b. sent " Trenches no 272 & came Cpl Gue & 5r. Ward signed on for further service.	
" 14	Sent no 2711 &7&15 15 &149 J.nos to replace deaths.	PAY
" 15	Routine.	
" 16	Sent in Report re suspended E. marked cases of Sr. Payne & Green. returns from late Shoeing Course. with certificate	
" 17	Lt. L.R. Williams attached to N.R.Batty. 2 horses Q.S. wagons detailed for R.E. Fatigue daily Cpl Tyreman from N.R. Rods refitted (Jointed) 1 himdrines SAA cart lent to 150" Inf. Bde.	
" 18	Capt. Savage R.A.M.C. reported for duty. Construction of new road to APieu begun with horses going daily down to Salter —	

Army Form C. 2118.

WAR DIARY
or
INTELLIGENCE SUMMARY.
(Erase heading not required.)

Instructions regarding War Diaries and Intelligence Summaries are contained in F. S. Regs., Part II and the Staff Manual respectively. Title pages will be prepared in manuscript.

Hour, Date, Place		Summary of Events and Information	Remarks and references to Appendices
RENNING-HELST	JANY. 1916		
G. 22. d 1x4	19	Attend 2 Soger Stones to BORRE 1 G.S vehicle left on TRANSPORT FARM broken down. (rear of Tanks)	
"	20	Provided 1 R.R Battery with A.S.C interCar. Brought in abandoned G.S wagon @ 7.P.M. damaged	
"	21	Sent a 1 R.R W. east to Bailleul Emerson saw W.O Engineers examining two shells recommended large Experiment left forest: Shells inoculated against Shrapnel.	PAY the instalist
"	22	Sent- 1 R. R.W east to STEENVOORDE for repair	
"	23	Sunday Shoeing horses with tin soles on a protective manner two wide - on advice of Vet Offr.	
"	24	Applied to C.R.A for ammun piercing S.A.A.	

(73989) W4141—463. 400,000. 9/14. H.&J.Ltd. Forms/C. 2118/10.

Army Form C. 2118.

WAR DIARY
or
INTELLIGENCE SUMMARY.
(Erase heading not required.)

Instructions regarding War Diaries and Intelligence Summaries are contained in F.S. Regs., Part II. and the Staff Manual respectively. Title pages will be prepared in manuscript.

Hour, Date, Place	Summary of Events and Information	Remarks and references to Appendices
RENNINGHELST JANY 25 1916 G.22.d.1.u.	Rushin	
" 26	Rushin	
" 27	New Road to Nordalus Completed	
" 28	Wrote to Adjt urging necessity of obtaining less fatiguing duties than getting horse & manure sufficient to R.E. 1 & 2 Res. reinforcements arrived at H.Q. from Bde.	Work to Front Trench picked up rails.
" 29	Field Sheer Complaints attached to 149. Sgt Nao. 16. Re-inforcements sent to Battalion. Pay.	PAY
" 30 Sunday	20 Reinforcements supplied to 1.2.12.Kistley for Special work. Ch. Parade.	

Army Form C. 2118.

WAR DIARY
or
INTELLIGENCE SUMMARY.
(Erase heading not required.)

Instructions regarding War Diaries and Intelligence Summaries are contained in F. S. Regs., Part II and the Staff Manual respectively. Title pages will be prepared in manuscript.

Hour, Date, Place	Summary of Events and Information	Remarks and references to Appendices
RENING HELST. G.22.d.1x4 JAN 31. 1916	Relieved 1st Battn. W Cork Run T Coy Walcstrs 6 have had extricated from post & defence was "MR.E. Gigue" but was on inhabited men to ward in 1 month been un-inhabited men.	6 N.C.O then go on leave during the month. no more arms issued during the month.
Summary "Amn" supplied during month	18pr All gun amm ready to A.C. t W. Lines. But Bi.w. ow except for supplied Watts - B'wrech supplied during the month to 149 Inf Bde - Ramis.	Generally quiet. daily Telegram including 6.9p. 4 heirs been dated to R.E. for each Trench meeting.
Gun 18pr Q.F. Rounds 912		Latrines - Balules Bundus filled Cook from to be erected -
S.A.A. amm. 319,000 Rounds	Ramps occasionally Bombed by Aero-planes + shelled - One man 1 A.E.J killed in action at KRUISSAART. during month. Health of Run + horses V. Good. ho nees fuses tit Better Waiscets leather Waistcoats.	Old + dangerous netting to be extracted in shots not Turn te Ethinel t haus Road evacuated. Three exiting tug of teams the cleared for fight mm is - Only L/B horse Should sup 1 must from + 57a creekshuh - Very Short of Amm Somany ammunition dagging was Gun Position.

Signed
CAPT. R.F.A. (T)
COMD'G. 2ND N.BRIAN AMM. COL.

(73989) W4141—463. 400,000. 9/14. H.&J.Ltd. Forms/C. 2118/10.

Confidential
War Diary
of
Lieut Col. H. W. Clapp
50th Divisional Ammunition Column
from 1/1/16 to 29/2/16.
Volume N° VII

WAR DIARY
or
INTELLIGENCE SUMMARY.

Army Form C. 2118.

Instructions regarding War Diaries and Intelligence Summaries are contained in F. S. Regs., Part II. and the Staff Manual respectively. Title pages will be prepared in manuscript.

(Erase heading not required.)

Place	Date	Hour	Summary of Events and Information	Remarks and references to Appendices
2½ miles S.W. of POPERINGHE	1/7/16		Nothing of interest to report beyond the usual routine duties	
	3rd/7/16 to 8/7/16			
	9/7/16		Nothing of interest to report	
	10/7/16		Collected 130 horses for Brigade Ammunition Column from CODEWAERSVELDE - loaded there over to the Brigades concerned	
	12/7/16		Enemy aeroplanes dropped several bombs in close vicinity to Camp without doing any material damage	
	13/7/16		Enemy aeroplanes again dropped considerable activity and again dropped bombs close to the Camp. Urgent demands for ammunition commenced to come in about 4. P.m. continued all night owing to assistance being called for by the 17th Division on our right - about 15 P.m. all these demands	
	14/7/16			

Army Form C. 2118.

WAR DIARY
or
INTELLIGENCE SUMMARY.
(Erase heading not required.)

Instructions regarding War Diaries and Intelligence Summaries are contained in F. S. Regs., Part II. and the Staff Manual respectively. Title pages will be prepared in manuscript.

Place	Date	Hour	Summary of Events and Information	Remarks and references to Appendices
2½ miles S.W. of POPERINGHE	14/7/16		were promptly met and no hitch occurred either in the supplying or delivering of ammunition	
	18/7/16		Enemy aeroplanes again active dropping bombs all round about the camp area.	
	20/7/16		Ditto	
	21/7/16		Ditto	
	14/7/16		Advanced Grenade store at KRUISSTRAAT hit direct, and set on fire, destroying about 4000 MILLS Grenades 1200 AVERY lights and 1000, NEWTON. PIPIN rifle Grenades	
	21/7/16		D.61. 4.5 Howitzer Battery transferred to the Division from the Guards Division	
	23/7/16		One Anti air craft gun (13 pounder) from the 17th Section arrived this placed in position in	

1577 Wt. W10791/1773 500,000 1/15 D. D. & L.   A.D.S.S./Forms/C. 2118.

Army Form C. 2118.

WAR DIARY
or
INTELLIGENCE SUMMARY.
(Erase heading not required.)

Instructions regarding War Diaries and Intelligence Summaries are contained in F. S. Regs., Part II. and the Staff Manual respectively. Title pages will be prepared in manuscript.

Place	Date	Hour	Summary of Events and Information	Remarks and references to Appendices
Vicinity of POPERINGHE	27/9/16		Headquarters filed.	
	28/9/16		Enemy aeroplanes again active in this area, but were unpleasantly surprised by the excellent shooting of the Anti Air Craft Gun under the command of Lieut Broad and quickly retreated to their own lines.	
	29/9/16		Lieut Sandilestone and 13 men from the Reserve Divisional Ammunition Column were transferred to this Unit.	

1577 Wt.W10791/1773 500,000 1/15 D. D. & L. A.D.S.S./Forms/C. 2118.

50

2 Northbran Am Col

Feb

Vol XI

Army Form C. 2118.

WAR DIARY
or
INTELLIGENCE SUMMARY.
(Erase heading not required.)

Instructions regarding War Diaries and Intelligence Summaries are contained in F. S. Regs., Part II. and the Staff Manual respectively. Title pages will be prepared in manuscript.

Hour, Date, Place	Summary of Events and Information	Remarks and references to Appendices
RENINGHELST.		
July 1st 1916	Capt. Fox Russell on leave. Lt. J.S. Broadbourne in charge of Amn. Col.	
G.22.d.1x4		
July 2	"C" Battery took down new main entrance R.E. Bridge girder transferred to M.T. Lorry. 7.9" Junker attacked NR Valley 2" Russ. point to Am. Col. 1" " 1.2 rds	
" 3	Rawlin	
" 4	Ref. for 10th June 30.13./2.E. (Change Ridle 7.46.	
" 5	Rawlin	
" 6	Rawlin	

WAR DIARY
or
INTELLIGENCE SUMMARY.

(Erase heading not required.)

Army Form C. 2118.

Instructions regarding War Diaries and Intelligence Summaries are contained in F.S. Regs., Part II. and the Staff Manual respectively. Title pages will be prepared in manuscript.

Hour, Date, Place	Summary of Events and Information	Remarks and references to Appendices
RENINGHELST FARM. May 7 1916 G.22.d.1x4	Zootijun to as usual	
" 8		
" 9	Routine as usual.	
" 10	Capt. Iw Smiths reported back from leave A.M. 10 A/C horses sent to Remounts CHESTRE.	
" 11	Transport lights inconveniently lit up adversely to the salient Tunnel horses. 10 A/C horses handed over to B.A.C.A. 21 A/6 horses arrived from base.	
" 12	Revd Eyld from Worthingham F. Sometimes Whitworth Yi. 10 A/C horses handed over to 17 Div. 4 A/6 ordered to relieve W/Xe Half. Batm.	

WAR DIARY
or
INTELLIGENCE SUMMARY.
(Erase heading not required.)

Army Form C. 2118.

Hour, Date, Place	Summary of Events and Information	Remarks and references to Appendices
REMINGHELST. Feb 13 1916 FARM. G.22.d.1x4 Sheet 28	Routine	
Feb 14.	Reported to 1/5 Argyles as to wounds as "delivery case". Sent B.T.O. 149 2nd Rdo W/o No T.32. to replace h/ 889. W/o sent Sheath & Cart Turning & the day. 2.45. wiring team talks came under very heavy shell fire at gas ahead. H.N.E. A shell burst in coach in front. 1 man Leary taylor in team wounds to 4 been immediately evacuated. 1 killed. 2 feet horses wounded. (Rev. 4r "BEATTY" wounded & left arm & eyes). evac. to 4 wounded at WINDEL "3 horses hit & sent to Mobile Vet 14/2/16. team had to be shot 11/2/16. Remainder sent to Mobile Vet the B.T. officer 149th Rdo reports W/o No 880. 27-3. hit & killed in team: should not have been — B. KAYE. wounded sent to hospital	"J wish to bring to your notice STARMSTRONG. 22/22 Iver last night 14/2 who behaved splendidly staying with the Gestation gettin even although the apparently acted
	Out Officer 6 pulverization gun upon a "where he evident was in which no. 195. under very heavy shell fire & H.R.E. burst. "hit him myself but I fear him the man "Also after he had never was hit the insisted & they had the Gunless apparently in getting him away Firing away all round him	with the greatest Coolness & bravery."

Army Form C. 2118.

WAR DIARY
or
INTELLIGENCE SUMMARY.
(Erase heading not required.)

Hour, Date, Place	Summary of Events and Information	Remarks and references to Appendices
RENINGHELST 1916 FARM G.22.d.14 July 15	750 Rounds A & A× 18 P. Gun ammunition drawn from B.A.C. & distributed to Batteries. Found 1 A/16 horse which [illeg] to 149 R.F.A. L.M.G. with other horses his number. A/16 2749 found on Road Sent to 'A' 74 (149 Bde) am ANN Ey horse shy (Unit was notified of 3 horses lost his No.) A/16. 149. Trade Referred 8/10 no. 2711 to treat list. BT.O. 149. Trade Referred for J. Shot 6 B/S [illeg] Lain in [illeg] Endey[?] 2746 killed A5V/S [illeg] Hurses Casualties [illeg] Gun fire 6 B/S own day Sent A/16 no 2753 & 8.50 to 149 D.Bde Cores away "item" Casualties No harvers. T. Officer Referred	
July 16.	19 Reinforcements H. Other arrived	
" 17	1 Recruit	

WAR DIARY
or
INTELLIGENCE SUMMARY.
(Erase heading not required.)

Army Form C. 2118.

Instructions regarding War Diaries and Intelligence Summaries are contained in F.S. Regs., Part II and the Staff Manual respectively. Title pages will be prepared in manuscript.

Hour, Date, Place	Summary of Events and Information	Remarks and references to Appendices
1916 RENINGHELST FARM. July 18 G.22.d.1.4 Sheet 28	6. Re intrenchments parties to Bm. HQ.	
" 19	BdeRemount inspected B/Brimers. Regt. & 2/L. Vaun succ firm 14 7 3. Rdrs & 2 drivers and Remounts a good firm constitution.	L. 6 horses 2/L. Vaun
" 20	Medium arc [illegible] that 2 i/c's + one. coy.	
" 21	Review	
" 22	parades w. HQ brim & R.V.G. pt 4 Field amb.	
" 23	Forces are to see B.A.S.A + QM Wagons lim trade.	

Army Form C. 2118.

WAR DIARY
or
INTELLIGENCE SUMMARY.
(Erase heading not required.)

Instructions regarding War Diaries and Intelligence Summaries are contained in F.S. Regs., Part II. and the Staff Manual respectively. Title pages will be prepared in manuscript.

Hour, Date, Place	Summary of Events and Information	Remarks and references to Appendices
Reninghelst Farm. Feby 24 1916 G.2.d.1×4.	All leave stopped. Handed over 2 M/G Team to 175 R.I.	
" " 25	No 1747 Sgt Scaife R. attached to "G" T.Mortar Battery	
" " 26	Orders received from Brigade 9.30 P.M. for six guns B.M. 10 & Sgt Davis & 12 men with him & Gunners reported from Base. A/Lt Wilson with C.O. sent to H.Q.s for training in gas school & no 7. Guns.	
" " 27	Recd. 1. 9.S S.a.gun. No. E.2476 from 9 & 4 from No.5. 7 Gunners Wynn Paraded 2 M/b times & 6 R. for Return Class School.	
" " 28	Routine.	Left Sect K.Belm e Poperinghe

WAR DIARY or INTELLIGENCE SUMMARY.

Army Form C. 2118.

(Erase heading not required.)

Instructions regarding War Diaries and Intelligence Summaries are contained in F.S. Regs., Part II and the Staff Manual respectively. Title pages will be prepared in manuscript.

Hour, Date, Place	Summary of Events and Information	Remarks and references to Appendices
Reninghelst 1/4 to Feby 29 B.2.2.d.1x4	2 2/Lts & Cloues transferred from 2 I.R. 10 to 7 Am. Col. transferred 2 L/Cpls provisional on H/Q for Return. Right Sect to Betho & Poperinghe	
	18 Gun Am. issued during the month. Rounds 16,520. "S.A.A. " " " S.4.6.50. Health of men good – Better on a week. Work – Fatigue for Engineers revetting in much damaged lines. Vehicles & horses up and army hire teams. Airplane activity much during unusual. 9 Bombs runs about Camp Koppernys with some bombardment of Busselsom. As many as 25 Kebeton out on Various fatigues in a day –	Weather during the month mild – Patched with 90% of the H/S horses in exchange for L.Q. 8-6 hour team work daily in fatigues. Batteries drawing Amn. direct from the R.R.S. – Improvement made to Camp accommodation and & Am. Park. 50 men on average away working for Railway – PS 1/4 –

Confidential

War Diary of
2 New Am Bde

1/A XII

AHSnade
Capt.

550

1/2 N bru B de R Ja
Au Col
Vol XII

Army Form C. 2118.

WAR DIARY
or
INTELLIGENCE SUMMARY.
(Erase heading not required.)

Instructions regarding War Diaries and Intelligence Summaries are contained in F.S. Regs., Part II and the Staff Manual respectively. Title pages will be prepared in manuscript.

Hour, Date, Place	Summary of Events and Information	Remarks and references to Appendices
RENINGHELST FARM MARCH 1st 1916 G. 22 d 1x4 Sheet 28	Recommends 1st ARMSTRONG for 16 C.N.I. for forming individuals went on 17 days leave. 10 Ro Inform ent arrived midnight Maltine.	
Do. 2		
4.20 A.M.	Very violent cannonading from British began north of Kelling Kalkhoff.	
10.10 A.M.	Rec'd phone message to send 3r men & all gun amn. wagon to KRSCH. B.S.W. MILHRA in charge.	9 A.M. sent 4 gt wagon in 12 Reg. trdy (4 miles in rear)
10.45 "	12 wagon left lines	
2.0 P.M.	The Amn. arrived at Billing W. Linie – 1 Sub: 4 wagon sent about up to gun calling at KRUISSTRAAT.	
4.35 "	Rec'd phone message from Adjt. Send every available wagon to B.S.E.L. to draw Amn.	
5.15	Sent off 8 GS wagons KRSCH unders/Whitehouse tomorrow 4 Team gun. 1st Nth Acn.	
6.30	S. of 1st 2 gun Amn. wagon ult applied 4 wgm has been return out gun to BUSERBOM	
8.30	Rec. msg by trucks. that 6 Gs wagon has been drawn gun stare. Jm a burnds being formed	
10.5 "	a dyst plum order for Gs team (which he drew out today) to proceed to OUDERBOM applying at B. Bde W Lim by 8 Wagm tues of Amn approved with Some to KRUISSTRAAT reporting there at 2 Me. x/a for a guide their am. up to gum	
10.30	The 8 Team left our lines under Sgt. Kirby.	

WAR DIARY
or
INTELLIGENCE SUMMARY.
(Erase heading not required.)

Army Form C. 2118.

Instructions regarding War Diaries and Intelligence Summaries are contained in F. S. Regs., Part II and the Staff Manual respectively. Title pages will be prepared in manuscript.

Hour, Date, Place	Summary of Events and Information	Remarks and references to Appendices
PENINGHELST. MARCH 2nd 1916 G. 22.b.1.4. 11.45 P.M. (continued)	The 8 GS. wagons ret^d located with 18pr SAA in Park of 25 Bngr. east Vlalel). Infantry reached Congested tunnels & St Hingh to Belleray to Lin under workmen. Run Ret. HQ. Barrel Vehicle above 7.4 Stragglers avoid @ W. Linn.	AX. 456.
Horsewith 149 S.SAA on loan — 25 with — 12 available (recluding 74) ___ L.B. am 111	Summary of Amm Collected from BAEs. A. 444 " OUSEBORM 608 " do. 698 wagn 400 __ 1452	300 __ 756
Ongs dailyRegy. Telign & Teams (4 by 2R)	to Issued. To W. Linn 1 2R. Btty 146 2 N.R. " 400 __ 148 1. Limber had to be left as 2 2RR Bty Guns with broken pole	104 300 252 __ 657
Leaving only 4 Teams for gun amm. Supply.	1 Wagon left at 113y posi in trees To Guns 1 2R Btty 304 2 454 __ 1452	100 __ 756
	2. Lt. W.E. Clarke reported for duty & am.ch .	

(73989) W.4141—463. 400,000. 9/14. H.&J.Ltd. Forms/C. 2118/10.

Army Form C. 2118.

WAR DIARY
or
INTELLIGENCE SUMMARY.
(Erase heading not required.)

Instructions regarding War Diaries and Intelligence Summaries are contained in F. S. Regs., Part II. and the Staff Manual respectively. Title pages will be prepared in manuscript.

Hour, Date, Place	Summary of Events and Information	Remarks and references to Appendices
RENINGHELST. Mch 3 1916 G.22.D.1x4	Resumed the hides to unwegen lyger.	Gun position reconnoiss.
" " 4	advise to A6V.3 resquins 3 6 4/5 Horses to bring knol. up to establishment	
" " 5	Gun Alignmt to R.E.	
" " 6	Do.	
" " 7	All men to Baths. 50% extra fuel to run edwin allowed. 1609. gv clark kelm s/3um. (officer arrive).	Men in Gun position

(73989) W4141—463. 400,000. 9/14. H.&J.Ltd. Forms/C. 2118/10.

Army Form C. 2118.

WAR DIARY
or
INTELLIGENCE SUMMARY.
(Erase heading not required.)

Instructions regarding War Diaries and Intelligence Summaries are contained in F.S. Regs., Part II. and the Staff Manual respectively. Title pages will be prepared in manuscript.

Hour, Date, Place	Summary of Events and Information	Remarks and references to Appendices
RENINGHELST. Mch 8. 13/6 G 22.d 1x4	Called Hell TFMs u Thurwell	
" 9	Reply re b cells for TFMs Hell Employment Survivors of daughter	
" 10	Tried forward a Reem Retn for ACI hen on night - enquirin Itlegm, during Parisher of serum involves s.m. Mullers Farvices in 4 unwilling line.	
" 11	Logging Daily 1/15 hun shelled - had to evacuate	mdant el- kreinstraat T
" 12	Logging Party out again at night serveras hu militarde.	

Army Form C. 2118.

WAR DIARY
or
INTELLIGENCE SUMMARY.
(Erase heading not required.)

Instructions regarding War Diaries and Intelligence Summaries are contained in F. S. Regs., Part II and the Staff Manual respectively. Title pages will be prepared in manuscript.

Place	Hour, Date	Summary of Events and Information	Remarks and references to Appendices
RENINGHELST	9.12.d.1.4 Mch 13	Made phone connection through Third Army Centre to C.R.A. R. Sec. & Popeninge Posit.	
	" 14	Detailed 2 Lt White + 1 Cpl. + 9 men for Course of T. mortar instruction. Left Sgt & Cpl Parker Staunton 24054 Munro 236.8 McArthur 3 reverted to drivers.	No 1372 Sgt Wilkins permanently
	" 15	New signalling school of 12 began. Wireless S/B completed from 14 Section. Capt Wade attached to A.Sec.	
	" 16	Fuller Mueller attached to N.R. 107.	
	" 17	Lt. J. Ness-Walker & Lt. Frank arrived at Division from Popeninge Station. Sapper Orm. Mancaster left for Base to be discharged.	

WAR DIARY
or
INTELLIGENCE SUMMARY.
(Erase heading not required.)

Army Form C. 2118.

Hour, Date, Place	Summary of Events and Information	Remarks and references to Appendices
RENINGHELST hch 18. 1916 9-22.d.1.4	Red from B.H.Q. 2.9. Remounts 4/6. Lt. R. Hunteman & 2 O.R.s arrived. Reports ex. 1 & 2 B.tty. Reinfo. 2.9 wagons ref. 15.5.16.	
" 19	Mr. G. Zanning (Intelpatz) Relge. reports back from leave. Branding & training new 4/horses. Ch. Parade.	
" 20	St. Kanken as before Co. Recd. 2. R. mounts. (Cut hens) from 1st & 2nd. Reports in Weirshyle Batterie came out of action after 9 hundits in. M. rotation withdrawn from Batty. WTwn.	
" 21		
" 22	Batty. holding In men applies for leave reformed Incidence. Johauns chilli awkward fourteen Harness Joranne ret. from 145 9. Bde Capt. Wade left in leave 8.45 AM. C + C. on Reconoghlst.	

Army Form C. 2118.

WAR DIARY
or
INTELLIGENCE SUMMARY.
(Erase heading not required.)

Instructions regarding War Diaries and Intelligence Summaries are contained in F. S. Regs., Part II. and the Staff Manual respectively. Title pages will be prepared in manuscript.

Hour, Date, Place	Summary of Events and Information	Remarks and references to Appendices
RENINGHELST 1916 C.22.d.1.4. Mch 23	New War Establishment issued - 12 officers change 4	Batts. Strength 29 145
" " 24	Authorised name for Tunnel Number 130th -	
" " 25	6 daily GS wagons to R.E. reduced to 2 wagons daily.	Bath
" " 26	Divisional ammunition to W.himan outside GS wagon there whilst end in return Wire T.F. Records York to J.S. Completed the Shimin Outergate	Bath Repairing Wagons
" " 27	12 wagon of Amm running all day filling up 2 858 vettes recommencing that guns upon to their new position.	Hoaiking Wheels
" " 28	Antiaircraft Complano to Bailleul & 2Amn Whirlup. Teams arrived back from gun position @ 7.30 AM.	20

Army Form C. 2118.

WAR DIARY
or
INTELLIGENCE SUMMARY.
(Erase heading not required.)

Instructions regarding War Diaries and Intelligence Summaries are contained in F.S. Regs., Part II and the Staff Manual respectively. Title pages will be prepared in manuscript.

Place	Hour, Date	Summary of Events and Information	Remarks and references to Appendices
REMINGHELST G.22.d.1x4 Sheet 28	1916 Meh. 29	Sent. 1 damaged 18 pr gun wagon to BAILLEUL wheelwrs. No time for leave.	Repairing, washing & painting vehicles. Harness shelters completed.
	" 30	2nd Lt. Ruwe reported from Hughens - Later gun +Rankin	Leave all washed & painted
	" 31	Ammunition issued during the month. 18pr Gun / A = 3040. / AX1812 = Total 4852 IR S.A.A. " 108,000 R².	
		Weather fine throughout the month very good. Steam engines & fatigues entailed many wheels & connecting rods & dr. Glenn proved indefinitely satisfactory. Rain (much) evening - Mh. Kindly teams of horses to Inf-ASC had wonderfully. They worked them unmercifully & their horse management various from bad to bad. They would not have lent must Regts one 25 L/b horses during the month to replace M/b taken away last month 50% of cases on their sick lines were cracked heels — gun weather according to Return disabled for 3 months. All obstinate cases - Forge Return not enough for horses doing so many

[signature] A.B. Smale
CAPT. R.F.A. (T)
COMD'g. 2ND N'BRIAN AMM. COL.

Confidential

WAR DIARY
or
INTELLIGENCE SUMMARY

2 New Arm[y] Corps

From 1.3.16
To 31.3.16

Vol. XII

Vol 849

Confidential

War Diary
of
Lieut-Colonel F.W. Cluff.

From 1.3.16 to 30.4.16.

(Volume 4)

50th Divisional Ammunition Column.

Army Form C. 2118.

WAR DIARY
or
INTELLIGENCE SUMMARY.
(Erase heading not required.)

Instructions regarding War Diaries and Intelligence Summaries are contained in F. S. Regs., Part II. and the Staff Manual respectively. Title pages will be prepared in manuscript.

Place	Date	Hour	Summary of Events and Information	Remarks and references to Appendices
POPERINGHE	1/3/16 to 25/3/16		Nothing to report beyond ordinary routine work. Establishment changed to that of the new lorries. The Column having three sections instead of four; resulting in an increase of Personnel and animals.	
GODEWAERSVELDE	4.4.16		The Column moved into Rest area at GODEWAERSVELDE.	
BERTHEN.	7.4.16		The Column moved to BERTHEN, to relieve the 2nd Canadian D.A.C. Nothing to report beyond ordinary routine work, with the exception of a night attack by the enemy. The Unit were able to supply all the ammunition that the Batteries demanded during the night, to meet this attack, without any hitch.	
	8.4.16 to 30.4.16			

H S Clark
Lieut Colonel
50th Divisional Ammunition Column

Army Form C. 2118.

WAR DIARY
or
INTELLIGENCE SUMMARY.
(Erase heading not required.)

Instructions regarding War Diaries and Intelligence Summaries are contained in F.S. Regs., Part II. and the Staff Manual respectively. Title pages will be prepared in manuscript.

Hour, Date, Place	Summary of Events and Information	Remarks and references to Appendices
RENINGHELST. APRIL 1916 G.22.d.1.4. 1	Routine	
" 2	All nominal Rolls shown to Lieut. Evans up to date	
" 3	Inspect 1 K.C. in full marching order. Huntsville	
" 4	Regt. Inst. 9 A.M. C.A. Struck Camp 6.0 A.M. & proceeded with S/4 & N.R. Battery to new area via Poperinghe. Abeele, Steenwoorde, & arrived in Camp at 2.30 P.M. Farm P.24.A.6.4. Sheet 27. Huntsville	1. Br. Q/... wagon sent 12R20/ 2 — A/S proceeding to Abeele 8 Officers
" 5	Capt. J.T. Woods Tour att. R.F.A. not duty with 2 & 12 R. Bty. Left Camp 9 A.M. Struck Camp. 9.0 A.M. & marched independently via Poperinghe Abeele. Reinforcements to join R. Sect 9 Guns arrived at 2.45 P.M. — in no. 18 Elcare	
Farm P.24.A.6.4. Sheet 27 " 6	Sgt. Strachan transferred from R.A. to N.R. Battery. Capt. Fletcher RAMC England on 4 week's leave. Dr. Hudson Officers to Huntsville	

(73989) W4141—463. 400,000. 9/14. H.&J.Ltd. Forms/C. 2118/10.

WAR DIARY
or
INTELLIGENCE SUMMARY.
(Erase heading not required.)

Army Form C. 2118.

Hour, Date, Place	Summary of Events and Information	Remarks and references to Appendices
1916 Farm M.21.c.1.8 April 7 Sh. 28 S.W.	Left Reck area for KEMMEL area. Staff to A.H.Q. (4, R & L Secs.) left P.24.a.6.4 at 8.30 AM & joined M4 & 13 Division at 9.30 - proceeded via SILVESTRE Cupola, CAËSTRE, FLETRE & BAILLEUL. Arrived MT VIDAIGNE at 12.30	Took my two duty relief horses in. 27 LOC (incl.) II Canadian Bro. & 44 all breakdown stopped on Lecem
" 8	A/Sgt Lundy acting Sgt Major in absence of S.M. Millward. 2 scout left 4 Am Col arrived at MT VIDAIGNE at 1.0 P.M. Practice bredeilli with 174 & Battery W. Lieu also B.T. Siphon Camp 15 U T. Md.	
" 9	15 Rd. 2nt Reinforcements arrived at Am. Col. purchase	
" 10	Men to Baths. Refr Winter Clothing Farriers B.S.S. Major Willard wanted office 4 weeks leave.	
" 11	Men to Baths. Driller Whiston sent to Base. He discharged Termination of Engagement	
" 12	Sgt Kirby & Dr Webster sent to Tubir Tunnel Mnts Rg for duty. R.E. 1380. Mule Grenades for Grenade Wynn & deleve. 762 Grenades returned 4 Billeton 15 Mar Tr. M.M. Battn.	

Army Form C. 2118.

WAR DIARY
or
INTELLIGENCE SUMMARY.
(Erase heading not required.)

Instructions regarding War Diaries and Intelligence Summaries are contained in F.S. Regs., Part II and the Staff Manual respectively. Title pages will be prepared in manuscript.

Hour, Date, Place	Summary of Events and Information	Remarks and references to Appendices
Mr Vidaigne 1916 April 13 M.21.C.1.2	Indian convoy empty 18th Am. Barrow Ferguson	
" 14	Impervia apparatus & Amm Dumps.	
" 15	Arranged with 150 Inds as General Supply.	
" 16	Routin	
" 17	Advance of Inn'ts Battery arrived & accommodated with A.S.C.	
" 18	Routin	

Army Form C. 2118.

WAR DIARY
or
INTELLIGENCE SUMMARY.
(Erase heading not required.)

Hour, Date, Place	Summary of Events and Information	Remarks and references to Appendices
MJH d'aigne M.21.c.1.2 **April** 19 28.SW	Attached officer St Johnston arrived at 14 chp course. Details of B battery left for gun drill. Forwarded W/T particulars of new "W.3" telephone — a very temperamental.	
" " 20	Routine	
" " 21	Further details from home arrived for B battery. Collected up B battery lines.	
" " 22	Major A.D.V.S. R.Vy Hanover who came to inspect for "debility" cases – but was unable to obtain authority for view.	
" " 23	Arranged special lines standing for horses suffering from debility. Easter Sunday. Early morning Celebration + Ch. Parade.	O i/c 37/4 & N.Z.V.y. O.P. 15. 9 Kennard sick.
" " 24	Easter Monday. Routine ½ day holiday.	

Army Form C. 2118.

WAR DIARY
or
INTELLIGENCE SUMMARY.
(Erase heading not required.)

Hour, Date, Place	Summary of Events and Information	Remarks and references to Appendices
M.I.V.B.R.I.G.N.S		
M 21.C.1.8 April 25 2.S.W	Diplomats kit to M.F. Officer BAILLEUL from BSth By Ammunition evacuated BSth from discharge.	Repairs Wagon Works " Painting "
" 26	Empties Amn. dump of all empty cylinders + Pieces. 18.95. 1PM Wdw used "Side of Special Vigilance"	
" 27	1.20 A.M. Stand to 4 – 5pm Rec'd unloaded some 4 military lorries am + 6 93 Wagons from B.A.C. Issued about 1600 Rounds in 3 hours. Kit + inspection of small arms, helmets, Rifles, artillery &	
" 28	Inventory Wagon Lines Reorganization &	
" 29	Passing Vehicles + Transport to Strike County for Rest Area. 8.10 P.M. Barn caught fire – discharges entire Permit thatcher Rest-House of Farm Spirits, in which was Farm dwelling [illegible] by driver. Rejoined with all horses taken to new Tramways in "I".1 and "5" for Attack on Ridge of the	Gas Alert followed Gas alarm. 9.30 P.M. Germs "E" "C" attack Vicinity of Annul.

WAR DIARY
or
INTELLIGENCE SUMMARY.
(Erase heading not required.)

Army Form C. 2118.

Hour, Date, Place	Summary of Events and Information	Remarks and references to Appendices

This is for Amn Issued during month the 2 Marie S'de concluded a period of 106 days in the line the Mnth the 2 Marie S'de concluded a period of 106 days in the Ypres Sahint taken with exception of 3 days a further Series of 24 days in action at KEMMEL specifically in Aspun area. Owing to being of 130 days — the Arras on Enemy out of Budedom — was in a four Enduron 12% being unreliable — the period at St Yen was + out our Very amiable reform & during the last 10 days twice the Inem enforcing sunline gas. Return of Enemy Recombins influence. Some shelle was remarkable ally under the what exceeds in the ten days. The Rain was unfue what exceeds in Italic & brought its effects hyst in the Stellmen in use. — Enemy gas attacks and but especially effective in the line Fugs.— It Aun Ct. was most startely perfect success occupied by the Ech — Pvt. Violaise — St Amn was amnunition seems SOS of the Grinm Btn— Battery for 3 days headfaces of ten hem's

Tui SAA issued

A = 57220
AX = 3242
= 2122
Runs =
= 103.000

[signature] Michaels
CAPT. R.F.A. (T)
COMD'G. 2ND N'BRIAN ARM. COL.

Confidential.

War Diary
of
Lieut-Colonel Cluff.

From 1.5.16 to 31.5.16.

Volume 7.

Divisional Ammunition Column.

50th Division.

WAR DIARY
INTELLIGENCE SUMMARY

Army Form C. 2118.

Place	Date	Hour	Summary of Events and Information	Remarks and references to Appendices
GODEWAERSVELDE	1.5.16 to 30.5.16		Unit moved from BERTHEN to rest area at GODEWAERSVELDE.	
	3.5.16		Unit entered G.H.Q. Reserve.	
	10.5.16		Re-organisation of the system of ammunition supply within the Division took place. G.H.Q. Letter No. O.B./818. The changed conditions consequent on the growth of the Army, and to provide an organisation which will be more manageable and more economical than that at present existing, the Commander-in-Chief has decided:- (a) To abolish the Bde Ammunition Columns. (B) To reconstitute the Div. Ammunition Columns into Div. Columns of two echelons, each composed as follows:- "A" echelon consisting of 3 Sections. "B" " " " of one Section. The Headquarters and "A" echelon are designed to accompany the Division closely at all times. "B" echelon will follow the Division if circumstances permit, but is detachable under Corps when necessary.	

WAR DIARY
or
INTELLIGENCE SUMMARY.
(Erase heading not required.)

Army Form C. 2118.

Place	Date	Hour	Summary of Events and Information	Remarks and references to Appendices
	30.5.16		Unit moved out of rest area, and proceeded to a position, two miles S.W. of KEMMEL.	
	31.5.16		Unit took over advanced Divisional Grenade Stores.	

H.P. Craig Lieut Colonel
50th Divisional Ammunition Column

Vol XI
50

"Confidential"

War Diary

of

Lieut-Colonel Cluff.

From 1.6.16 to 30.6.16.

Volume X

D. A. C. 50th Division.

WAR DIARY

INTELLIGENCE SUMMARY

Army Form C. 2118.

Place	Date	Hour	Summary of Events and Information	Remarks and references to Appendices
Mt NOIR.	1-6-16 to 30-6-16	3rd	Four mules were killed by shrapnel ↠ Kemmel, while engaged on fatigue duty with the engineers. B. Wales, in charge of the party, showed great presence of mind, and by his example and efforts, saved further casualties to his men and mules.	
		10	Thirty thousand rounds of ammunition were delivered by the Park to the unit, followed by a further eight thousand on the 18th. This was dealt with in a very successful manner by the sections.	
		13.	B. Wales was awarded the Military Medal for his conduct, and the fine example he set to his men, when under shell fire on June 3rd.	
		14	On 18/6 wagon-body, containing H.E. Shells, blew up, on the 2nd Rouge - de - noir, road, which taking up ammunition. The gunner, sitting on the wagon, was extremely wounded, and one mule was slightly damaged. Considering the force of the explosion, it was remarkable that there were not more casualties. Cpl Rotsen in charge of the party, showed great coolness in getting his men and mules clear of the fire. His prompt action averted a further	
		16	and in putting out the fire. His prompt action saved a further	

Army Form C. 2118.

WAR DIARY
INTELLIGENCE SUMMARY

(Erase heading not required.)

Place	Date	Hour	Summary of Events and Information	Remarks and references to Appendices
			explosion and further casualties. He was amongst the Infantry which drove them in. An enquiry was held, to ascertain the cause of the explosion, but no conclusion could be arrived at. Twenty one thousand rounds of ammunition were delivered to the unit.	

Vol 12

CONFIDENTAL

WAR DIARY

of

LIEUT. COLONEL F. W. CLUFF

50TH DIVISIONAL. AMMUNITION COLUMN

FROM 1ST JULY TO 31ST JULY 1916

VOLUME ~~16~~

WAR DIARY
INTELLIGENCE SUMMARY

Army Form C. 2118.

Place	Date	Hour	Summary of Events and Information	Remarks and references to Appendices
Mont Noir	July 1-4		Nothing of importance to record.	
Westoutre	5-31.5		"A" Echelon moved into new and unprepared billets on the Westoutre - Reninghelst road. Inspite of the short notice, the sections were clear of their lines by the appointed time, the move being successfully accomplished.	
		6th	"B" Echelon moved into the field at Westoutre, previously occupied by "A" Echelon of "A" Echelon. The 24th D.A.C. took over the ammunition dumps left by this unit.	
		8th	The 24th D.A.C. left the area. This unit took charge of the ammunition dumps and removed same to "A" Echelon.	
		12th	Preparations were made to receive and deal with large quantities of ammunition at the railway sidings at OUDERDOM.	

Army Form C. 2118.

WAR DIARY
—or—
INTELLIGENCE SUMMARY.
(Erase heading not required.)

Instructions regarding War Diaries and Intelligence Summaries are contained in F. S. Regs., Part II. and the Staff Manual respectively. Title pages will be prepared in manuscript.

Place	Date	Hour	Summary of Events and Information	Remarks and references to Appendices
WESTOUTRE	July.	14.	Six 15 P.R guns, carriages, and limbers were collected by the 2nd Section, and parked in "A" Echelon.	
		18.	The 15 P.R guns, carriages, and limbers were collected by the 24th D.A.P.	
		25.26.	Forty eight wagons from 'A' and 'B' Echelons collected gas cylinders from R.E. Farm and R.E. Dump. During this operation confusion and great delay was caused owing to the highly unsatisfactory manner in which the cylinders were brought up, and handed over to the officer in charge of the wagons.	
		27.	A confirmation service was held in the Convent at Locre, by the Bishop of Khartoum. Five men from this unit were confirmed.	
		28	Fifteen wagons, thirty horses, heavy draught, and fifteen drivers were attached to this Unit, to relieve the strain put upon "A" and "B" Echelons, by the heavy fatigues they have been called upon to perform.	

1577 Wt. W10791/1773 500,000 1/15 D. D. & L. A.D.S.S./Forms/C. 2118.

WAR DIARY
INTELLIGENCE SUMMARY
(Erase heading not required.)

Army Form C. 2118.

Place	Date	Hour	Summary of Events and Information	Remarks and references to Appendices
WESTOUTRE	July 31.31		"A" Echelon. The condition of the horses in three sections comprising this Echelon leaves much to be desired. On reorganisation, the horses handed over by different Units were, in a large majority of cases, in a very debilitated and poor condition. Some improvement has been obtained by careful treatment, but the very dry shower fences on this Unit, as a whole, in throwing fatigues has severely handicapped the building up of horses. Fully 60% of which, are entirely unfit for anything, that completi. rest and special treatment when when given. The horses in "B" Echelon, which were handed over by the Sections of "A" Echelon on change of establishment, are in excellent condition, although the heavy day and night fatigues they have had to perform. These animals have been frequently under shell fire, not equally at night, and in no case has there been any stampede, or trouble of any kind with them.	

Y.S. Carey
Lieut Colonel
O.C. Divisional Ammunition Column

Vol 13

CONFIDENTIAL

WAR DIARY.

OF

Lieut. Colonel F. W. Cluff.

50th Divisional Ammunition Column.

FROM 1:8:16 TO 31:8:16.

VOLUME ~~17~~.

Army Form C. 2118.

WAR DIARY
or
INTELLIGENCE SUMMARY.

(Erase heading not required.)

Instructions regarding War Diaries and Intelligence Summaries are contained in F. S. Regs., Part II. and the Staff Manual respectively. Title pages will be prepared in manuscript.

Place	Date	Hour	Summary of Events and Information	Remarks and references to Appendices
WESTOUTRE	August 1-9		During this period the Unit was not called upon to perform the same number of fatigues as it was during the latter part of July. The amount of ammunition supplied was also considerably less. The opportunity was taken to clean & repair the wagons, & improve the horses as far as possible.	
GODEWAERSVELDE	" 9-12		The Unit came out of action on the 9th and proceeded into the Rest Area at GODEWAERSVELDE. Preparations were made for the entraining, and heavy marching which was shortly to take place	
"		K.R.R. 11-12-13	Operation Order attached. The Unit entrained as follows :- Headquarters and 3rd Section at GODEWAERSVELDE. 1st and 2nd Section at BAILLEUL. Right half "B" Echelon at GODEWAERSVELDE. Left half at BAILLEUL. The 1st and 2nd Sections entrained during the nights of 10-11th and during the 11th The left half of "B" Echelon on the morning of the 12th. The 3rd Section during the night of 11th-12th. Headquarters on the morning of the 12th and the Right half "B" Echelon on the afternoon of the 12th.	No. 1

Army Form C. 2118.

WAR DIARY

or

INTELLIGENCE SUMMARY.

(Erase heading not required.)

Instructions regarding War Diaries and Intelligence Summaries are contained in F. S. Regs., Part II. and the Staff Manual respectively. Title pages will be prepared in manuscript.

Place	Date	Hour	Summary of Events and Information	Remarks and references to Appendices
			The Section which entrained at BAILLEUL, detrained at DOULLENS, and marched to BOISBERGUES. The remainder detrained at CANDAS, and proceeded to BOISBERGUES. The entraining and detraining throughout the unit was carried out promptly and keenly, special attention being paid to punctuality. During the journey itself, nothing remarkable occurred.	
BOISBERGUES	12-13-14		The Unit rested here before proceeding further South.	
BOURDON			The Unit left BOISBERGUES at 4.30 on the morning of the 15th, and marched to BOURDON; the route being via BERNAVILLE, BERNEUIL, PERNOIS, and VIGNACOURT. Distance 18 miles. Operation Order attached.	No. 2
"	14-15th		BOURDON was reached by mid-day on the 14th. One hour after arrival orders were received, to be in readiness to move to FRECHENCOURT in a few hours	

1577 Wt.W10791/1773 500,000 1/15 D. D. & L. A.D.S.S./Forms/C. 2118.

Army Form C. 2118.

WAR DIARY
or
INTELLIGENCE SUMMARY.
(Erase heading not required.)

Place	Date	Hour	Summary of Events and Information	Remarks and references to Appendices
	15th		The Unit left BOURDON at 2.15 A.M., and marched to FRECHENCOURT, via VIGNACOURT, VILLERS BOCAGE, MOLLIENS-AU-BOIS. Distance 18 miles. The tail of the Column was past the AMIENS - DOULLENS road by the appointed time 8.30 A.M., and FRECHENCOURT was reached by 10.30 A.M. Both this, and the march of the previous day were accomplished without trouble of any kind. Operation Order attached.	No. 3.
FRECHENCOURT	15th-17th		During this period as much rest as possible was given to the men, horses and mules.	
ALBERT	18th, 19th		This Unit relieved the 34th. D.A.C. by hay Echelons. "A"+ "B" Echelons left FRECHENCOURT at 7.30 A.M on the 18th and marched to ALBERT, via BAIZIEUX, HENENCOURT, and MILLENCOURT, and took over the camp previously occupied by the 34th D.A.C. situated 500 yards North West of ALBERT. Operation Order attached.	No. 4.

Army Form C. 2118.

WAR DIARY
or
INTELLIGENCE SUMMARY.
(Erase heading not required.)

Instructions regarding War Diaries and Intelligence Summaries are contained in F.S. Regs., Part II. and the Staff Manual respectively. Title pages will be prepared in manuscript.

Place	Date	Hour	Summary of Events and Information	Remarks and references to Appendices
	19th		The remainder of the Unit, less the left half of "B" Echelon moved to ALBERT.	
	20th		The right half of "B" Echelon less ten wagons, and No.1 Section "A" Echelon returned to FRECHENCOURT	
	21st		Large quantities of ammunition were supplied to the Batteries	
	22nd		The camp was removed to a position 800 yards due West of ALBERT, and dump was constructed on the ALBERT - AMIENS road, on account of enemy shells falling in close proximity to the dump.	
	23-28th		The supply of ammunition continued to be of large quantities. A cover for the dump was commenced, but was interfered with by the rain storm which swept over the camp during the 29th and 30th.	

H.S. Crump
Lieut Colonel
50th Divisional Ammunition Column
31/8/16.

SECRET

50TH DIVISIONAL AMMUNITION COLUMN.
No. ....
Date. 7/8/16

Operation Order No 1.

1. The 50th D.A.C will be relieved by the 19th D.A.C on Wednesday 9th inst.

2. The Sections will be relieved by half sections. The relief to be completed by 12 noon, times of marching later.

3. The D.A.C. will march to rest area via, WESTOUTRE, Mt. KOKEREELE, BOESCHEPE, Road junction R.1.d24 - GODEWAERSVELDE.

4. Positions in rest areas are as follows:-
   - Headquarters.   Q. 18. a. 5. 5.
   - 1st Section.   Q. 10. d. 9. 7. ⎫
   - 2nd -"-   Q. 23. a. 4. 4. ⎬ Sheet 27.
   - 3rd -"-   Q. 17. b. 6. 9. ⎭
   - 4th -"-   { Q. 6. d. 0. 1.
                      { Q. 12. b. 3. 8.

5. All units will move out on relief with all Echelons full to establishment with ammunition. Surplus ammunition will be handed over to relieving Units. Amount handed over to be reported to this office as soon as relief is completed.

6. All camp equipment according to lists forwarded will be handed over, & receipts, according to "Pro Forma" sent to this office.

7. Reports on completion of relief to be at once sent to Headquarters.

8. Acknowledge.

[signature]
CAPTAIN & ADJUTANT.
50th DIV. AMMUNITN. COLUMN.

OPERATION ORDER No 2
14-8-16.

1. The 50th D.A.C., will march to BOURDON to-morrow as follows.

(a) Headquarters will pull out into dust road below 2° Section ground at 4-0am & feed.

(b) The 3rd Section will pull out on to road leading from BOISBERGUES - BERNAVILLE so that rear wagon is clear of junction with LE MEILLARD Road at 4-10am.

(c) Headquarters will move off at 5.0 am, followed at 200 yds interval by 3rd Section, followed at same interval by 2° Section, followed at same interval by 1st Section, followed at same interval by 4th Section.

(d) The route to be taken, Rd. junction just North of 1st E of BERNAVILLE - BERNEUIL - PERNOIS - Rd. junct. 1 mile West of V of VIGNACOURT - North of FORET DE VIGNACOURT - N of BOURDON.

3

(e) Head of Column will not move South of ~~line through STOU~~ BERNEUIL before 7·45 am.

(f) The column must be South of line through STOUEN-LAVICOGNE by 10-0 am

(g) On arrival on point referred to in (e) the distances between sections will be closed up to 100 yards.

2. A Billeting party consisting of 2/Lt. Clarke, Sergt. Scott & 1 N.C.O. or gunner from each Section, all with bicycles & rationed for 15th – 16th will parade at new Headquarters BOURDON at 1·05 pm, to join S.6. at VIGNACOURT at 2·30 pm

3. O.C. Sections will see that all drag ropes are handy on wagons.

4. Acknowledge.

F. Moor Armstrong
Capt & Adjt

50. D.A.C.

Copy No 1. Secret

Operation Orders no 3 15-8-16

1. Unit will move tomorrow to FRECHENCOURT via VIGNACOURT, VILLERS BOCAGE, MOLLIENS AU BOIS.

2. Headquarters leave at 2-15 a.m
   3rd Section 2-25 a.m
   1st ----   2-35 a.m
   2nd --   2-45 a.m
   4   --   2-55 a.m

3. Tails of Column to be EAST of the main road AMIENS – DOULLENS by 8-30 a.m.

4. Intervals of ½ mile to be kept between Bdys & D.A.C.

5. On arrival in new billeting area the greatest care must be taken to keep the road clear.
   No Horses are to be sent to water out of horse lines until all units are in their lines.

   F. Stonehouse Capt
   Adj 5o D.A.C

6. [illegible]

7. Acknowledge.

1 Table.

Copy No. 1. to 1st Section
 "   " 2 " 2 "
 "   " 3 " 3 "
 "   " 4 " 4 "
 "   " 5   H.Q

Copy No. 5   SECRET.

OPERATION ORDER No 4.

1. 50th D.A.C. will relieve 34th D.A.C. on the 18th & 19th days: the former to passing at railhead on the 19th.

2. Half Sections will march in the order & date as W2/y Sept 57 D.

3. Under the three nights as preceded the half sections will march each day as one unit at 11.0 am in following order:- 1st section 2nd Section 3rd Section, 2nd Section, Capt. Vaughan being in charge of half column on the 18th & Capt. Wakeman on the 19th.

4. Route to be taken via BEHENCOURT - BAIZIEUX - HENENCOURT - MILLENCOURT

5. The Ammunition left by sections of the 34th D.A.C. to be taken over by Sections of the 50th D.A.C. & will be to be up to the W.E. ready for action at 1.0 pm on the 19th.

50th. DIVISIONAL ARTILLERY

50th. DIVISIONAL AMMUNITION COLUMN

SEPTEMBER 1916.

Vol 14

CONFIDENTIAL.   30. 9. 16.

WAR DIARY

of.

LIEUT-COLONEL CLUFF.

COMMANDING D.A.C. 50 DIVISION.

From September 1st to September 30th.

VOLUME ~~7~~

Army Form C. 2118.

WAR DIARY
INTELLIGENCE SUMMARY.
(Erase heading not required.)

Instructions regarding War Diaries and Intelligence Summaries are contained in F. S. Regs., Part II. and the Staff Manual respectively. Title pages will be prepared in manuscript.

Place	Date	Hour	Summary of Events and Information	Remarks and references to Appendices
ALBERT. 1-8.	September 2.		The covering, and the roads for the Ammunition dumps, on the ALBERT-AMIENS road, were completed.	
	3.		A dug-out was built for gas-shells, which were delivered to this Unit for the first time. One man was killed, one wounded, four mules killed, two wounded, and a G.S. wagon damaged, by shell fire on the CONTALMAISON-BAZENTIN road.	
	4.		1st Section relieved the 3rd Section; the latter proceeding to FRICOURT.	
	6.		Third Corps reserve ammunition dump on the ALBERT-MILLENCOURT road was put under the charge of an Officer, four N.C.O.s and sixteen men detailed from this Unit.	
	7.		Throughout this period the amount of ammunition issued to the Brigades continued to be large. The total number of rounds of A.P.[?] amounting to thirty five thousand, five hundred, and sixty two. One hundred and sixty gas shells were also delivered.	
	8.		On Sept. 1st, and at intervals up to Sept. 7th, the camps, horse lines,	

Army Form C. 2118.

WAR DIARY
or
INTELLIGENCE SUMMARY.
(Erase heading not required.)

Instructions regarding War Diaries and Intelligence Summaries are contained in F.S. Regs., Part II. and the Staff Manual respectively. Title pages will be prepared in manuscript.

Place	Date	Hour	Summary of Events and Information	Remarks and references to Appendices
BECOURT WOOD 8-9D			heavy guns, and main roads in the immediate neighbourhood were shelled by 4.2 and 5.9 guns, shooting from the direction of THIEPVAL. On Sept 8th shelling again started at 11.30 A.M. The first shell fell fifty yards in front, and to the right of the camp, the second thing twenty yards short; All horses and men were immediately cleared off the ground and drawn up, five hundred yards down the ALBERT - AMIENS road. The shelling continued for two hours, several shells falling in the camp. The casualties from this unit were reported, and the material damage was slight. Three men, and some horses were killed in the next camp. At 2.30 p.m. orders were received to move Head Quarters, the 1st, 2nd, and advanced portion of the 4th sections to a new position in BECOURT WOOD, F.I.B. Sheet 62 D. The remaining part of the unit to remain at FRECHENCOURT. The move was completed by 8.0 P.M. The evacuated camp was again shelled during the night, the following day, and at intervals during the following week.	

WAR DIARY
INTELLIGENCE SUMMARY

Army Form C. 2118.

Place	Date	Hour	Summary of Events and Information	Remarks and references to Appendices
BECOURT WOOD	9.		A new dump was started on the new BECOURT-CONTALMAISON and FRICOURT road. The 2nd Section and the returned portion of B echelon, less 28 G.S. Wagons moved back to MILLENCOURT to D.S.a. Sheet 62.D. The 3rd Section moved from FRENCHENCOURT to MILLENCOURT. Operation order attached.	No. 5.
	10-12		Material removed from the ALBERT dump, and reconstructed at the BECOURT dump.	
	13.		O.C.'s 2nd and 3rd sections joined Head Quarters at BECOURT WOOD, with all their 18 P.s and 4.5 ammunition wagons, leaving their S.A.A. Sections at MILLENCOURT, attached to O.C. B echelon for administration and discipline. A railway line running up to BECORDEL was extended up the valley to the dump; after which, ammunition was delivered by train direct to the dump.	
	14		The demands from the Brigades for ammunition exceeded all previous records. Over twelve thousand rounds being issued during the day.	

Army Form C. 2118.

WAR DIARY
INTELLIGENCE SUMMARY.
(Erase heading not required.)

Place	Date	Hour	Summary of Events and Information	Remarks and references to Appendices
BÉCOURT WOOD	15.		This ammunition was used on the following day, by the batteries, during the successful attack on MARTINPUICH, COURCELETTE, and FLERS. The remaining portions of the 2nd and 3rd sections moved from MILLENCOURT to BÉCOURT.	
	19		B Echelon moved from MILLENCOURT to BÉCOURT. The heavy rain which fell throughout the previous day, continued during the 19th and the morning of the 20th, increasing to a very great extent the difficulties of transport.	
FRICOURT WOOD 20-30	20.		The Unit moved to a new position between LONELY COPSE and FRICOURT WOOD. F. 3. b. 8.7. Sheet 62. D. Operation order attached. A new dump was made on the road running along the north west side of FRICOURT WOOD.	No. 6.
	21.		Further difficulties were encountered by the transport working in forward areas, owing to the bad state of the ground. The G.S. wagons engaged in carrying stone to the new roads, running	

WAR DIARY

INTELLIGENCE SUMMARY.

(Erase heading not required.)

Army Form C. 2118.

Place	Date	Hour	Summary of Events and Information	Remarks and references to Appendices
FRICOURT.	22-25.		Though BAZENTIN and HIGH WOOD suffered particularly heavy damage, Sloc being temporarily placed out of action in one day. The condition of the horses and mules at this period was beginning to cause considerable alarm. Fortunately, owing to a decrease in the number of fatigues, which B echelon was called upon to perform, and the demands for ammunition becoming considerably smaller, a much needed rest was able to be given to the horses. The weather conditions also improved considerably.	
	28.		During this period, several points in the neighbourhood, more especially FRICOURT WOOD, and the camp on the east side of LONELY COPSE were shelled at intervals. Bombs were also dropped in the vicinity by hostile planes on two occasions, each time during the night. Tear Shells, on one occasion fell for a period of two hours, on a point about five hundred yards north east of the camp. At 11.15 A.M. on the 28th it was considered advisable to move all horses from the lines, owing to the shelling of FRICOURT	

Army Form C. 2118.

WAR DIARY

or

INTELLIGENCE SUMMARY.

(Erase heading not required.)

Place	Date	Hour	Summary of Events and Information	Remarks and references to Appendices
FRICOURT.	28.		WOOD. The shelling continued for forty five minutes. No shells fell the camp, one fell a few yards from the dump, but no damage was done.	
	29.		The Officer, N.C.O's and men, in charge of the Third Corps reserve ammunition dump reported the Unit.	
	30		One man belonging to B Echelon was killed at HIGH WOOD whilst employed on Stone fatigue.	
			During this month the ammunition issued to the Brigades by this Unit exceeded all previous records. The total number of rounds supplied amounting to two hundred and twenty three thousand.	
			During this period under review, Officers and O.R.'s of this Unit have all worked under exceptional and at times, conditions of considerable danger. With the utmost coolness and resource, the whole working of the unit, proceeding without any hitch or delay in carrying out the demands of Ammunition made on them.	

J.A. Clift
Lieut Colonel

Operation Order. No. 6.   19.9.16.

Head Quarters, and all sections will move to 1:3. b. 87.
and ground West of that road.
Section Commanders will make their own
arrangements. Will move to later place at 9.0. a.m.
C.O. will allot the ground at 9.30 a.m..
Lieut. Clarke and party at Dump will remain
here until further orders.

Operation Order No 5.   9.9.16.

The unit less, Headquarters, 1st Section,
28 G.S. Wagons from 4th Section, complete
horse ants and necessary details, will march
at 9.0 A.m. on 10th September to Camp D. E.S.y

VOLUME. 18.   October 1916.

Vol 15

WAR DIARY
of
LIEUT-COLONEL CLUFF.
COMMANDING

D. A. C.
50. DIVISION.

From October 1 — to October 31.
1916.

VOLUME ~~18~~

Army Form C. 2118.

WAR DIARY
INTELLIGENCE SUMMARY.
(Erase heading not required.)

Place	Date	Hour	Summary of Events and Information	Remarks and references to Appendices
FRICOURT. 62.D. F.3.b.	October 1st to 31st		From the experiences of the last six weeks of an entirely new kind of warfare, the Unit had learnt what is of importance, and to what most attention must be given to make troops as efficient as possible under the new conditions, with the result that early during this month a distinct improvement was noticeable in the general work, and in the condition of the men and horses.	VOLUME 18.
	1.		Hostile aeroplanes dropped bombs on camps in the vicinity. Several horses were killed.	
	2.		Nine horses sent to H.Q. 251 Bgde to replace casualties caused on the previous night by bombs from enemy aeroplanes.	
	3.		C.R.A. 50th Division, relieved by C.R.A. 23rd Division. 253 Bgde, and infantry also relieved.	

Army Form C. 2118.

WAR DIARY
or
INTELLIGENCE SUMMARY.
(Erase heading not required.)

Instructions regarding War Diaries and Intelligence Summaries are contained in F. S. Regs., Part II. and the Staff Manual respectively. Title pages will be prepared in manuscript.

Place	Date	Hour	Summary of Events and Information	Remarks and references to Appendices
	4.		The quality of the rations issued to this Division at this period was giving just cause for complaint.	
	5.		Owing to continuous bad weather since the beginning of the month, operations on this front were considerably impeded, which rendered the calls for ammunition light. Only two thousand, five hundred rounds were supplied on the 2nd, and two thousand, three hundred on the 3rd.	
	6-7.		The weather conditions improved. Calls for ammunition increased.	
	8.		Demands for ammunition continued to be heavy. Fourteen thousand rounds were supplied on this date.	
	10		One man wounded, one man killed and eight severely wounded (apparently) whilst engaged on a stone fatigue in MARTIN PUICH.	

1577 Wt. W10791/1773 500,000 1/15 D. D. & L. A.D.S.S./Forms/C. 2118.

Army Form C. 2118.

WAR DIARY
of
INTELLIGENCE SUMMARY.
(Erase heading not required.)

Instructions regarding War Diaries and Intelligence Summaries are contained in F. S. Regs., Part II. and the Staff Manual respectively. Title pages will be prepared in manuscript.

Place	Date	Hour	Summary of Events and Information	Remarks and references to Appendices
	11.14 15.		Nothing of importance to report. Stables for the winter commenced by H.Q.s and each section.	
	16		At this period from three thousand to four hundred cartridge cases were being collected daily by this Unit, and were returned by the R.S.P. to the next Base.	
	17.		Preparations were made to open a new dump at PEAKE WOOD STATION, on the FRICOURT - CONTALMAISON road. Owing to the railway junction at BOTTOM WOOD being shelled during the night, it was impossible to get ammunition up by rail. The allotment for the 17th was delivered according to of the old dump at FRICOURT WOOD, by lorry.	
	18.19 20		Ammunition continued to be delivered at FRICOURT. Officers i/c of the Dumps, and men withdrawn from PEAKE WOOD.	

WAR DIARY
INTELLIGENCE SUMMARY.
(Erase heading not required.)

Army Form C. 2118.

Place	Date	Hour	Summary of Events and Information	Remarks and references to Appendices
	21-23			
	24		Work on the stables carried on. One man wounded. One mule killed through explosion of a hill hand grenade lying on the ground partly covered, to the camp. One hundred and twenty gas shells issued to the batteries. The infantry returned into action.	
	25-27		Demands for ammunition fairly light, only the 253 and the 253 Bgdes being in action.	
	28		The fatigues are found very heavy. In addition to the regular daily fatigue of twenty seven G.S. wagons, wagons were detailed for the transport of grenades. The carting of the material for the stabling from G. dump also necessitated the use of several wagons daily. On this date sixty eight G.S. wagons and lorries were on the road.	
	29-31		The weather conditions, which have been remarkably poor during	

Place	Date	Hour	Summary of Events and Information	Remarks and references to Appendices
	31.		The whole month now seemed very bad, making several roads almost impassable. Eight horses to each wagon was found necessary on several days. This caused much to be postponed, most especially by the 92nd section, supplying ammunition direct to the batteries.

The total number of rounds supplied by this unit during this month amounted to one hundred and seventy eight thousand nine hundred & ninety. Therefore fell short of two months fire by forty five thousand. This is due to the fact that during the earlier part of the month, there [were?] only two were in action, and during the latter part, only two. The average amount supplied to each Bgde during October screens the average for Bgde for September, by seventeen thousand round. This is a remarkable occurrence, seeing that there was considerably more activity on this front during September. | |

Now in October, after two weeks of heavy and continuous work, signs of fatigue begin to be seen in both the men and horses are clearly to be seen. Though this is the case, the unit has been able to deal with all the shipments for ammunition, and to perform a large number of fatigues daily, successfully. The strain during the coming month will probably be thoroughly greater, and the resources of the Unit will be taxed to the highest degree. Evidence of overwork, and of billets quite unsuitable for the weather is seen in the daily numbers of men who report sick, and are unfit for duty.

[signature]
Lieut Colonel

Army Form C. 2118.

50th DIV. Am Col

Vol: II   November 1916

WAR DIARY
~~INTELLIGENCE SUMMARY~~
(Erase heading not required.)

Instructions regarding War Diaries and Intelligence Summaries are contained in F. S. Regs., Part II. and the Staff Manual respectively. Title pages will be prepared in manuscript.

Place	Date	Hour	Summary of Events and Information	Remarks and references to Appendices
NOVEMBER FRICOURT	1st			
"	2		Eleven men wounded on the previous evening by the explosion of a bomb dropped by an enemy plane on one since died. Owing to the continuous bad weather great difficulty was experienced in getting wagons of any description over the forward roads. The wagon lines and Sections supplying down to the guns found it quite impossible to get even limbered up to the batteries and now resorted to supplying ammunition by pack horses. On this date a convoy of wagons left the dumps at 7 am to deliver ammunition in MARTINPUICH, & did not return until 8 pm	
"	3rd		Heavy rain continued to fall. FRICOURT WOOD & CIRCUS heavily shelled from 1 pm to 4.15 pm. They could suffered no casualties.	
"	4th		The following awards to NCOs and Men of the unit were announced :-	
			No. 12113 BQMS Young J. Meritorious Service Medal	
			" 24 Gunner Hynard J.E. do	
			" 509 Driver Payne R do	

WAR DIARY
or
INTELLIGENCE SUMMARY

Army Form C. 2118.

Place	Date	Hour	Summary of Events and Information	Remarks and references to Appendices
FRICOURT	4ᵗʰ (cont)		N° 207 Bomb. Oxley A.A. Meritorious Service Medal	
			„ 2133 Serg.ᵗ Kirby S.R. Military Medal	
			do do do Bar to Military Medal	
			N° 205 Bomb. Nash A.H. Military Medal	
			N° 363 Bomb. McGahan J. do	
			N° 117 Gr. Kennedy T. do	
			N° 567 D°. Wildgoose E do	
			N° 390 „ Trotter J do	
	5ᵗʰ		The number of men reporting sick daily is considerably on the increase. This is due to the billets being totally unsuited to the adverse weather conditions.	
	7ᵗʰ		The number of fatigues performed daily by A and B Echelons very high.	
	8ᵗʰ		Over sixty G.S. Wagons on road work from this Unit. Owing to the bad state of the roads, & the fact that only two	
	9/10ᵗʰ		Brigades 250ᵗʰ & 253ʳᵈ were in action the demands for ammunition	

WAR DIARY

Place	Date	Hour	Summary of Events and Information	Remarks and references to Appendices
	9/10 (contd)		were small.	
	11th		FRICOURT CIRCUS shelled during the night. 250th & 253rd (Northumbrian) Brigades came out of action.	
	12th		No more ammunition supplied.	
	13th		Orders received to prepare to hand over to IIAC 23rd Division	
	14th		The Unit was relieved by 23rd DAC at 1.30pm and marched eastward ALBERT, along the main ALBERT-AMIENS road through LAHOUSSOYE & BEAUCOURT. 1st Section proceeded to FRECHENCOURT, 2nd & 3rd Sections to BEHENCOURT. "B" Echelon to LAVIEVILLE. The move was accomplished satisfactorily. The roads before ALBERT were reached were very heavy, but improved considerably after ALBERT was passed. OPERATION ORDER attached. Thirty thousand rounds of ammunition were supplied during November, making the total since August 20th, under the Division came into action on this front, up to five hundred thousand rounds.	No 7.

Army Form C. 2118.

WAR DIARY
or
INTELLIGENCE SUMMARY.
(Erase heading not required.)

Instructions regarding War Diaries and Intelligence Summaries are contained in F. S. Regs., Part II. and the Staff Manual respectively. Title pages will be prepared in manuscript.

Place	Date	Hour	Summary of Events and Information	Remarks and references to Appendices
BEAUCOURT	15"		The casualties suffered by the Unit have been remarkably light, when the nature of the work undertaken is taken into consideration. Three men, and ten mules having been killed. Ten men + ten mules having been wounded. One man deeply wounded received.	
	16"		"B" Echelon at LAVIEVILLE called upon to do twenty fatigues daily at CONTALMAISON. Distance considered too great.	
	18"		1st Section moved to MOLIENS-au-BOIS. HQ joined 1st & 2nd Sections at BEHENCOURT. Arrangements made to park Wagons and Animals of 4th Section working on forward area, at BOTTOM WOOD. Crew having 12 miles for day	
	22		Arrangements made to take over from the 9th T.M.C at BECOURT; and thew dump at BOTTOM WOOD	
	24		The Unit marched from BEHENCOURT via HENENCOURT, MILLENCOURT and ALBERT to the positions previously occupied by the 9th T.M.C, two thousand yards from ALBERT on the FRICOURT—	

Army Form C. 2118.

WAR DIARY

(Erase heading not required.)

Place	Date	Hour	Summary of Events and Information	Remarks and references to Appendices
BECOURT	25 28		ALBERT road, & took over from that about at 2pm, also the Ammunition Dump at BOTTOM WOOD. Camp found to be in a very dirty condition. Demands for ammunition very light.	OPERATION ORDER attached No 8

Moore Armstrong Capt

for OC 55 Dn Am Col

OPERATION ORDER No 9

50th Divisional Ammunition Column

Copy 5

1. The 50th DAC will move on Wednesday 6th inst, to position now occupied by 23rd DAC at X 27 d

2. Times of move as follows:—

Headquarters	11 am
1st Section	11.5 "
2" -"-	11.20 "
3" -"-	11.35 "
4" -"-	11.50 "

3. The Sections will be harnessed up ready for inspection by O.C. half an hour before the scheduled times for moving off.

4. An officer will inspect the present billets before leaving, & O's 6 Sections will render a certificate to Headquarters Office as soon as possible after arrival in new area that their old billets have been so inspected, & left clean. If necessary fatigue parties must be left to clean up.

5. The Sections will occupy billets now occupied by the corresponding Sections to their own in 23rd I.A.C.

6. Headquarters, & each Section will send representatives forward to new area, to arrive not later than 9 am on the 6th inst, to take over the new billets. Lists of stores taken over to be forwarded to Headquarters Office.

7. The present Billets will be handed over to the 48th Division, each Section leaving a representative behind to do this. All scheduled Huts, Tents, Bivouac Covers, Tarpaulins, etc, taken over by this Unit from the 9th Division, or since issued to Sections, must be handed over to the incoming Unit. Receipts taken in duplicate, to be forwarded to Headquarters Office.

8. All Ammunition & Grenades now in possession of the Sections will be taken with them to the new area. If it is not found possible to move same with the Unit, owing to shortage of Transport, a guard must be mounted over same, & transport sent back to collect the balance. Guard will not be relieved until all ammunition has been removed.

Army Form C. 2118.

50TH DIVISIONAL AMMUNITION COLUMN

DECEMBER 1915

WAR DIARY

INTELLIGENCE SUMMARY.

(Erase heading not required.)

Instructions regarding War Diaries and Intelligence Summaries are contained in F. S. Regs., Part II. and the Staff Manual respectively. Title pages will be prepared in manuscript.

Vol: XI   No 17

Place	Date	Hour	Summary of Events and Information	Remarks and references to Appendices
	DECEMBER 1916			
BECOURT	1-5		Nothing of importance to report	
FRICOURT	5-31		The Unit moved to FRICOURT and took up the same position which it had left on being relieved by the 23rd D.A.C. on Nov. 12th.	OPERATION ORDER ATTACHED No 9.
			During their occupation of the camp the 23rd D.A.C. had not done anything towards the improvement of the camp. No attempt had been made to make the stables or huts, preparing it for winter conditions. No attempt had been made to other and in several cases material drawn for the above purpose had been used for other things. Trenches dug on either sides of the stables for drainage purposes had been filled up with manure. Timber forming a road to the dumps, remainder of the camp had been pulled up, & had disappeared.	
			Plans laid down for change of the camp. Work started on stables, huts &c. During the remainder of the month, the work of constructing huts, stables, digging drains was carried on, & all hands working at high pressure.	
			Supply of ammunition very small, in comparison with the previous months.	

HSElliott
Lieut Collier

WAR DIARY

INTELLIGENCE SUMMARY

Army Form C. 2118.

50TH DIVISIONAL AMMUNITION COLUMN

VOLUME No. XIII   JANUARY 1917   Vol 18

Place	Date	Hour	Summary of Events and Information
FRICOURT	1/1/17 to 31/1/17		The drainage of the camp & stables has been carried on & with very satisfactory results. The work has been very hard for the men, but the fore the end of the month nearly all the horses were on proper standings & under cover; & of course all N.C.O. & men had been hutted. Owing to having to send 150 horses to refill batteries, the efficient working strength of the D.A.C. has been much impaired. This was effected by the middle of the month. Also on 18.1.17 as the whole D.A.C. had to go through a process of reorganisation, accomplishment of detail was naturally very much hindered as they were reduced by the officers, over 100 men and over 90 horses. The 80 horses which were sent down from batteries were and are practically useless, and they may be rather of help (on paper) to the Co Column. The strength of the Column is below the instant. Head Quarters & Echelon Lines (with the exception

Army Form C. 2118.

WAR DIARY
or
INTELLIGENCE SUMMARY.

(Erase heading not required.)

Instructions regarding War Diaries and Intelligence Summaries are contained in F. S. Regs., Part II. and the Staff Manual respectively. Title pages will be prepared in manuscript.

Place	Date	Hour	Summary of Events and Information	Remarks and references to Appendices
MIRVAUX	29/11/17		H. "B" Echelon were taken over by the 1st Australian D.A.C. Everything was most satisfactory. "B" Echelon is due to arrive at our present H.Q. today.	Operation Order No 10.
	3/11/17		On the march through ALBERT on 29/11/17 the town was shelled attacked by the Germans with heavy shells, on two occasions the H.Q. Column very narrowly escaped, two shells falling within a few yards of it. There were however no casualties.	

H J Clay
Lieut-Colonel
Commanding
50th Northumbrian D.A.C.

Operation Order No. 10
50th Divisional Ammn Column.
28-1-17.

1. 50th DAC. will be relieved by 1st Australian DAC on January 29-30th and February 1st. and will move to rest billets at MIRVAUX.

2. Route will be by ALBERT - LAHOUSSOYE - BEHENCOURT - MOLLIENS-au-BOIS. - MIRVAUX.

3. Times of moving off:-

January 29th   Headquarters   6.0 a.m.
                 2nd Section   6.15 "
January 30th   1st Section   6.15 "
February 1st   B Echelon   6.15 "

Sections to parade on road outside camp $\frac{1}{4}$ hour before above times.

4. Road Control, Halts, etc.   Last vehicle to be clear of ALBERT by 8.0 a.m. First road halt at X roads — (LAVIEVILLE) where horses will be watered and small feeds put on. Leading vehicle not to enter BEHENCOURT till 12.0 noon. If an extensive halt is necessary outside BEHENCOURT, feeds should be put on.

2.

5. ROAD INTERVALS

50 yards between Headquarters & Sections (or between Sections) Sections will move in Sub-sections of 6 vehicles. The last vehicle of each 6 to carry the white disc on the near side. The rear vehicle of a section will carry a double disc. See Divisional Order QX/4673/1 of 25/1/17, for position of discs on vehicles.

6. REAR PARTIES

O'C 1st & 2nd Sections will each detail a rear party of 1 NCO & 6 men to remain behind to clear up the camp and disinfect the Stables. Particular attention to be paid to this latter point. These parties will report to Captain H.L. MEAGHER, and will travel with 'B' Echelon on Feb., 1st.

O'C 'B' Echelon will see that his camp is left clean & stables disinfected before departure.

O'C Sections will render a certificate to Headquarters Office that their camp was left in a clean condition.

3

7. COMMAND   On departure of Headquarters, Captain MEAGHER will take over command, and will hand over to 1st Australian DAC.   On arrival at MIRVAUX he will report to Headquarters.

8. BILLETING   A billeting party of 1 NCO per Section with bicycles will report to the ADJUTANT at TOWN MAJORS. OFFICE, MOLLIENS-au-BOIS at 10 am on 29th Jan.

9. BAGGAGE WAGONS will not be available.

10. LOAN OF TEAMS (a) O6 'B' Echelon will lend O6. No 2 Sections 3 teams complete to move with 2nd Section on 29th inst. These teams will be returned on 30th inst with an additional 8 teams which will then remain with 'B' Echelon and assist it to move to rest area.

(b). 66 B Echelon will lend 66 No 1 Section 4 teams complete to move with 1st Section on 30th inst, & will remain with 1st Section until arrival of B Echelon at rest area.

4.

(c). OC No 1 Section will lend Headquarters 1 G.S. Wagon & team C.T.O. on the 29th inst to assist Headquarters to move. The wagon should be sent to Headquarters at once

SUPPLIES:-

11 (a) "B" Echelon will draw double rations + forage on 30th inst for consumption on 31st and 1st February

(b) Supply wagons will travel with Sections. They should be unloaded + sent back to No 1 Coy immediately on arrival.

(c) Supply Dump in rest area will be at PIERREGOT.

H.O. Clupp
Lieut Colonel

28/1/17

Army Form C. 2118.

WAR DIARY
or
INTELLIGENCE SUMMARY

(Erase heading not required.)

PAGET

Place	Date	Hour	Summary of Events and Information	Remarks and references to Appendices
MIRVAUX	1/2/17 to 4/2/17		"B" Echelon duly arrived at MIRVAUX. Considerable difficulty was experienced in obtaining billets and horse lines. The former when obtained were very ill suited to the arctic conditions of weather then prevailing and the men suffered considerably from the cold.	
	5/2/17		Orders were received to move to VAIRE. The Column this time moved as a complete Unit with the exception of 19 wagons belonging to "B" Echelon. Teams were not available for these owing to shortage of animals, and to having to provide teams to help the batteries to move. A guard was left in charge of these wagons and teams were sent back the following day to bring them on. The Unit arrived at VAIRE without any trouble or mishaps occurring on the route.	Operation orders No. XI attached.
VAIRE	6/2/17		As the men had had no chance of having any recreation	

50th Divisional Ammunition Column
Operation Order No. 12. Copy No. 6
11-2-17

1. The 50th D.A.C. will move to the forward area as under:—
   Headquarters ⎫
   1st Section   ⎬ 12th inst

   2nd Section ⎫
   'B' Echelon ⎬ 13th inst
   252nd Bde HQ ⎭

2. Route for party moving on 12th will be via HAMEL – CERISY – MORCOURT – R.33 a

   Route for party moving on 13th will be via VILLIERS BRETONNEUX – WARFUSSE – R.33 a.

3. Times of moving off will be as under.
   Headquarters   9 am   12th inst
   1st Section   9.10 am do
   2nd Section   9.0 am 13th inst
   B Echelon   9.15 "   do
   252 Bde HQ   9.30 "   do

4. ROAD CONTROL. 12th inst. Head of Column to halt at entrance to HAMEL at 9.30 am & to follow D/251. 13th inst. Head of Column to halt at entrance to VILLERS BRETONNEUX

2

at 10.15 am, & follow C/251 at proper interval

5. ROAD INTERVALS

The following Road Intervals will be strictly observed. White discs will be used as before

Between Sections   200+ $\dagger$
Between Sub sections   25+

6. COMMUNICATION   Two cyclist orderlies per Section will be detailed for the march. One to ride in front of the Section and one in rear.

Any delay or stoppage of traffic will be reported at once to the Section Commander and to the C.O. at the head of the Column. An officer <u>must</u> invariably remain at the head of a Section and after a halt must be prepared to move immediately an order to march reaches him.

7. LOAN OF TEAMS (O.)

O.C. "B" Echelon will lend O.C. N° 1 Section 2 teams for the 12th and O.C. N° 2 Section 2 teams for the 13th inst. These teams will be handed over under

3.

mutual arrangements.

The "G.S. Wagon & team at present with HQ" from 1st Section will march with Headquarters.

LOAN OF TEAMS (b)

8. On arrival at the forward area O.C No 1 Section will return to 'B' Echelon, the 2 teams lent to him and in addition 7 additional teams, rations for 48 hours to be taken.

9. REAR PARTIES. O.C. Sections will render a report to the Adjutant on arrival at the forward area that all billets and horse lines in VAIRE were left in a clean and sanitary condition.

10. WATERING en ROUTE.

No arrangements are necessary for watering animals en route, but buckets will be available for this purpose on arrival at the destination

11. ACKNOWLEDGE.

HW Clupp
Lieut. Colonel.
Comdg 50"D.A.C

Copies To:-

1. Headquarters
2. 1st Section
3. 2nd Section
4. B. Echelon
5. 252nd Bde Hdqtrs
6. War Diary.

SECRET.

50th Divisional Ammunition Column
Operation Order No 11 Copy No 6
4-2-17.

1. 50th D.A.C. will tomorrow 5th inst march to billets at VAIRE.

2. Route will be by PIERREGOT - MOLLIENS-au-BOIS - ST GRATIEN - FRECHENCOURT - PONT NOYELLES - DAOURS - AUBIGNY - FOUILLOY - HAMELET - VAIRE.

3. Times of moving off will be:-
   Headquarters   7.30 am.
   1st Section   7.45 "
   2nd   "   8.0   "
   B Echelon   8.15 "
   252 Bde HQ   8.30 "

4. ROAD CONTROL   Head of column to cross river at DAOURS at 11.30 am. Rear of column to have crossed by 2 pm. III Corps is given priority of use of above route. Normal traffic must be allowed to circulate. No long halts will be made North of the SOMME.

5. ROAD INTERVALS   The column will march as a Unit. Intervals between Sections 200 yards, and between sub-sections 25 yards. While dries will be carried as before. Proper intervals must be maintained along the whole march.

6. COMMUNICATION   At least 1 cyclist orderly will march at front, and another at rear of each Section. Any undue delay or block in traffic will be at once reported to Section Commanders, and to Adjutant at head of Column.

7. LOAN OF TEAMS   (a) O.C. B Echelon will lend O.C. No 1 Section 4 teams & O.C. No 2 Section 2 teams complete. These teams should be handed over under mutual arrangements, and will be returned on arrival at VAIRE.   (b) The G.S. Wagon & team at present with Headquarters from 1st Section will march with Headquarters.

3

8. SURPLUS VEHICLES   The following
Surplus vehicles will be collected
by O.C. N° 2 Section, & left parked
in his present wagon park.
     6. - 18 pr Limbered Ammn wagons
     1. - G.S. Technical Wagon.
                              In addition
O.C. B Echelon will park empty, in
the same place this afternoon all
G.S. Wagons on his charge for which
he cannot provide teams. The
number thus left will be reported
at once to this office.

9. REAR PARTIES
                              A rear party
of 1 N.C.O. & 3 men from each Section
will remain behind to clean up
billets and to mount guard over
vehicles left behind. These men
will have 3 days rations in
possession.
                              This party
will parade at Headquarters
Office tonight at 5.30 pm for
instructions.

4.

10. WATERING ON ROUTE.   This will not be possible, but O.C. Sections will see that buckets are ready for watering on arrival.

11. COPIES TO:
   1. Headquarters
   2. 1st Section
   3. 2nd Section
   4. B Echelon
   5. 252nd Bde. Hdqrs.
   6. War Diary.

12. ACKNOWLEDGE

Capt. & Adjt.
50th D.A.C.

Army Form C. 2118.

WAR DIARY
~~INTELLIGENCE SUMMARY~~

50th DIVISIONAL AMMUNITION COLUMN

February 1917 VOLUME XXIII Page 1 Vol/9

Place	Date	Hour	Summary of Events and Information	Remarks and references to Appendices
VAIRE	6/2/17		For several months opportunity was taken to arrange a series of football competitions between the sections. This was successfully carried out and was much appreciated by the men who considerably benefitted by the relaxation after their long spell of continuous and heavy work.	
VAIRE	11/2/17 to 13/2/17		Orders were received to move to the forward area. Headquarters and "A" Echelon moving on the 12th and "B" Echelon on the 13th. This move was very satisfactorily accomplished.	Operation order No XII attached
	14/2/17 to 28/2/17		Nothing of importance to report beyond ordinary routine work.	

H.C. Clunn
Lieut Colonel

WAR DIARY
INTELLIGENCE SUMMARY.
(Erase heading not required.)

50th DIVISIONAL AMMUNITION COLUMN.

VOLUME XXIV   MARCH 1917   Vol 2

Army Form C. 2118.

Place	Date	Hour	Summary of Events and Information	Remarks and references to Appendices
PROYART	1.3.17 to 20.3.17		Nothing of importance to report.	
	21.3.17		The Unit moved to VAIRE-SUR-CORBIE, being relieved by the 59th D.A.C. on March 21st, 22nd & 23rd. Great difficulty was experienced by officers left behind at PROYART to endeavour, in getting the relieving S.A.C. to take over from them, delay being caused in this way, & also because of the fact that the in-coming S.A.C. had orders to find accommodation for the whole unit in PROYART village, & expected our officers to point out & clearly order they were to. Our 2nd section had orders reported to be very dirty, & the landing over officer of this section was ordered to have the huts cleaned out in spite of the fact that men of the 59th Division had been using these huts for the two days previous to the relief taking place.	Operation order No. XIII attached
	22.3.17 23.3.17		Fourteen G.S. wagons were sent to batteries for this move.	
	26.3.17		The Unit moved to HAVERNAS (a distance of over 20 miles) together with the whole of the D.A. It is interesting to note, that during the whole of this march, the animals were neither untied nor fed, units being unable to do so, having orders to be clear of VILLERS-BOCAGE by 11 A.M. It was impossible	

Army Form C. 2118.

WAR DIARY

INTELLIGENCE SUMMARY.
(Erase heading not required.)

Instructions regarding War Diaries and Intelligence
Summaries are contained in F. S. Regs., Part II.
and the Staff Manual respectively. Title pages
will be prepared in manuscript.

Place	Date	Hour	Summary of Events and Information	Remarks and references to Appendices
			to carry out the latter, owing to congestion of traffic.	Operation order No. XIV attached
HAVERNAS	28.3.17		One animal was destroyed on this march. Twenty four G.S. wagons were lent to batteries for this move.	
BOISBERGUES	29.3.17		The unit moved to BOISBERGUES.	Operation order No. XV attached. Operation order No. XVI attached.
			The unit moved to HUMBERCOURT.	
			Two animals were destroyed on this march.	
HUMBERCOURT	30.3.17		The unit moved to MONCHIET, to be transferred from 3rd corps Fourth Army to XVIII Corps Third Army & being temporarily attached to VII Corps.	Operation order No. XVII attached
			Two animals were destroyed en route.	
MONCHIET	31.3.17		The Unit commenced the delivery of ammunition to the batteries.	

H.C. Clinch
Lieut-Colonel
commanding
50th (Northumbrian) D.A.C.

S E C R E T.   Copy No 6

Operation Order No 13 by Lieut Col F.W.CLUFF.,R.F.A.(T)
Commanding 50th Divisional Ammunition Column.

1. 50th D.A.C. will be relieved by 59th D.A.C. on March 21st, 22nd and 23rd, as under :-

    2nd Section 'A' Echelon,   21st March, passing Starting
                                Point at 9.0 a.m.

    1st   "   "   "   22nd March, passing Starting
                                Point at 7.30 a.m.

    Headquarters,   )
    'B' Echelon   )   23rd March, passing Starting
    & 252 Bde H.Q.   )   Point at 9.0 a.m.

    Starting Point is Cross Roads at R.26.d. (SUCERIE).

2. Route will be by WARFUSEE-VAIRE. Best route between WARFUSEE and VAIRE should be reconnoitred, but road by HAMEL is not to be used.

3. The following road intervals will be observed :-

    Between Sections and Headquarters.   200 yards.
       "   Sub-Sections.   25 "

    White tail discs will be used.

4. Loan of teams to batteries.

    'A' Echelon will detach the following G.S. Wagons (C.T.Os.) to batteries over the move :-

    2nd Section. 7 G.S.Wagons to 250 Bde on 21st.
                    reporting at Wagon Lines at 3 p.m.
    1st Section. 7 G.S. Wagons to 251 Bde on 22nd,
                    reporting at Wagon Lines at 3 p.m.

    These wagons will accompany batteries and will go on to VAIRE after delivering loads (one journey only).

    A Sergeant will be in charge of wagons attached to each Brigade.

5. Two days rations and forage to be carried.

6. AMMUNITION.

    Sections of 'A' Echelon will move full, with Gun Ammunition, ~~S.A.A. and Grenades~~ only.

    S.A.A. and Grenades will be handed over to relieving unit.

    'B' Echelon will dump ammunition carried by the 22 Wagons which are being sent to BOIS L'ABBE in a convenient place for lorries. Eleven lorries will report at Cross Roads (SUCERIE R.26.d.) at 8. a.m. on 23rd instant. An Officer or senior N.C.O. should meet them and guide and give necessary orders for loading. These lorries will take the ammunition to VAIRE and report to Officer in charge of teams already there.

6. **REAR PARTIES.**

   A rear party of 1 N.C.O. and 4 men will be left by each Section to disinfect stables, and clean up billets. The 'A' Echelon parties will assist the 'B' Echelons on the 23rd and 24th and all will be collected on the 24th instant by 2nd Section. 3 days rations will be left in each case.

7. One Officer per Section will remain behind attached to corresponding Sections of 59 D.A.C. for two days, to assist them

   These Officers will also render certificates to Headquarters on return as follows :-

   (a) Cleanliness of Billets. and SAA & Grenades
   (b) Disinfection of Stables.
   (c) Receipts for Corps Stores handed over.

   These Officers will return under Section arrangements.

8. **BILLETING.**

   Sections will send an N.C.O. the day before they move to report to 2nd Lieut CLARKE at VAIRS.

   O.C. 'B' Echelon will have the Billeting Certificates for his Unit and Headquarters 282nd Brigade prepared and signed by the O.C. and finally by the MAIRE on the 22nd instant.

9. ACKNOWLEDGE.

   D. Hay

   Capt.
   Adjutant 50th Divisional Ammunition Column.

Issued   20th March, 1917.

Copy No 1.   1st Section.
      2.   2nd Section.
      3.   'B' Echelon.
      4.   282nd Bde H.Q.
      5.   War Diary.
      6.   Spare.

SECRET.   Copy No 5

Operation Order No 14 by Lieut Col F.W.CLUFF, R.F.A. (T)
Commanding 50th Divisional Ammunition Column.

1.   50th Divisional Ammunition Column will move to
NAVESNES and WARSNES, on March 26th, 1917.

2.   Starting Point :-   Road Junction VAIRE.
J.32.a.20 Sheet 57D.

3.   Order of March :-

Headquarters.   Head of Column to pass Starting Point
                   at 5.45 a.m.
1st Section.   Head of Column to pass Starting Point
                   at 5.48 a.m.
2nd Section.   Head of Column to pass Starting Point
                   at 6.3 a.m.
'B' Echelon.   Head of Column to pass Starting Point
                   at 6.18 a.m.
250 R.F.A.(H.Q.) Head of Column to pass Starting Point
                   at 6.30 a.m.

        Unit will be clear of VILLERS BOCAGE by 11.0 a.m.

4.   ROUTE :-

CORBIE BRIDGE - CORBIE - QUERRIEU - ALLONVILLE -
COISY - VILLERS BOCAGE - FLESSELLES - HAVERNAS.

5.   MARCH DISCIPLINE :-

The distance between Sections will be as laid down in
F.S. Regs Part I., i.e., 10 yards.

White discs will be on the rear vehicle of each
Section.

Officers and Nos 1 will ride on the off side of their
teams.

6.   LOAN OF TEAMS TO BATTERIES :-

'A' Echelon will detach the following G.S.Wagons
(G.T.Gs.) to Batteries for the Move.

1st Section. 6 G.S. Wagons.   251 Brigade R.F.A.
                                The Wagons having been
                                detached already the teams
                                will report as detailed
                                to 251 Bde H.Q. at 4.10 a.m.

2nd Section. Ditto.   Ditto.

'B' Echelon. 12 G.S. Wagons to 250 Brigade R.F.A.,
distribution as follows :-

6 (Continued)　　H.Q. 250 Bde.　　1 G.S. Wagon.
　　　　　　　　A/250 Bde.　　　2 " "
　　　　　　　　B/250 Bde.　　　3 " "
　　　　　　　　C/250 Bde.　　　3 " "
　　　　　　　　D/250 Bde.　　　3 " "

　　The wagons having been detached already, the teams
will report as detailed as above at 4.10 a.m.

7.　　AMMUNITION :-

　　Echelons will dump all ammunition at V.25.d.5½.
Sheet 57D, and move empty.

　　The Guard detailed to look after the ammunition
will remain until it has been removed. Three days
rations will be left with this party.

　　Orders for N.C.O. of Guard are sent direct to him.

8.　　BILLETS :-

　　All billets must be left clean and in a sanitary
condition, before departure. A certificate to this
effect being rendered to this office by 5 a.m.

9.　　REFILLING POINT :-

　　Refilling Point for Supplies will be at FLETCHERS.

10.　　ACKNOWLEDGE.

　　　　　　　　　　　　　　　　　　　　2nd Lieut.
　　　　　　　　　　　for Adjutant 50th Divnl Amn Column.

8th March, 1917.

Issued at 10.0 p.m.

Copy No 1.　to　1st Section.
　"　 "　2.　"　2nd　"
　"　 "　3.　"　'B' Echelon.
　"　 "　4.　"　250 Bde H.Q.
　"　 "　5.　"　War Diary.
　"　 "　6.　"　Spare.

SECRET.   COPY NO. 5

Operation Orders No 15 by Lieut Colonel F.W.CLUFF R.F.A.(T)
Commanding 50th Divisional Ammunition Column.
----

1. 50th D.A.C. will move to BOISBERGUES on March 28th 1917.

2. ORDER OF MARCH.

	Time of leaving billets.
Headquarters	10-35 am.
2nd Section	10-47 am.
3rd Section &)	
252 Bde H.Q.)	10-59 am.
1st Section	11-11 am.

3. Route will be by CANAPLES - MONTRELET - FIENVILLERS - AUTHEUX.

4. March Discipline
   White discs will be on rear vehicle of each Section.

5. AMMUNITION.
   Echelons will move empty.

6. BILLETS
   All billets must be left clean and in a sanitary condition before departure. A certificate to this effect being rendered to this Office by 10 am.

7. REFILLING POINT
   Refilling point for supplies on 28th inst will be at HEM.

8. Acknowledge

                                                    2Lieut
               for Adjutant, 50th Divisional Ammunition Column.

Issued at 7-0pm. 27th March 17.

Copy No 1.   1st Section.
        2.   2nd Section.
        3.   'B' Echelon.
        4.   252 Bde H.Q.
        5.   War Diary.
        6.   Spare.

SECRET   COPY NO 5.

OPERATION ORDER NO 16 BY LIEUT COL F.W. CLUFF. R.F.A.(T).
COMMANDING 50TH DIVISIONAL AMMUNITION COLUMN.

1. 50th Divisional Ammunition Column will proceed to HUMBERCOURT and COULLEMONT on 29th March, 1917.

2. STARTING POINT   Church, BOISBERGUES.

3. ORDER OF MARCH --
   Headquarters.   Head of Column pass Starting Point
                                         at 7.15 a.m.

   'B' Echelon
   & 252 Bde H.Q.   "   "   "   pass Starting Point
                                         at 7.18 a.m.

   1st Section.   "   "   "   pass Starting Point
                                         at 7.35 a.m.

   2nd Section.   "   "   "   pass Starting Point
                                         at 7.52 a.m.

4. ROUTE --
   OUTREBOIS - OCCOCHES - DOULLENS - LUCHEUX.

   All Units 50th Divisional Artillery are to be clear of DOULLENS by 11.0 a.m.

5. MARCH DISCIPLINE --

   A distance of 500 yards will be maintained between each Section.

6. AMMUNITION --

   Echelons will move empty.

7. BILLETS --

   All Billets must be left clean and in a sanitary condition before departure.
   A Certificate to this effect being rendered to this office by 6.45 a.m.

8. ACKNOWLEDGE.

                                          J Dean   2nd. Lieut.
                    for Adjutant 50th Divisional Ammunition Column.

Issued at 10.45 a.m.

Copy No 1.   1st Section.
 "   " 2.   2nd   "
 "   " 3.   'B' Echelon.
 "   " 4.   252 Bde H.Q.
 "   " 5.   War Diary.
 "   " 6 & 7. Spare.

Ref: Map LENS, Sheet 11, 1/100,000.   SECRET

                                                 Copy No 4

OPERATION ORDER NO 17 BY LIEUT COL F.W.CLUFF., R.F.A.(T).
COMMANDING, 50TH DIVISIONAL AMMUNITION COLUMN.
----

1. 50th Divisional Artillery is being transferred from Fourth Army to Third Army (XVIII Corps). It will be attached temporarily to VII Corps.

2. 50th Divisional Ammunition Column will proceed to WAILLY on 30th March, 1917.

3. Starting Point - Cross Roads 500 yards N. of B in HUMBERCOURT.

4. ORDER OF MARCH --

   Headquarters.   Head of Column pass Starting Point at 9.15 a.m.
   1st Section.   "   "   "   "   Starting Point at 9.18 a.m.
   2nd Section.   "   "   "   "   Starting Point at 9.35 a.m.
   'B' Echelon.   "   "   "   "   Starting Point at 9.52 a.m.

5. ROUTE --

   COUTURELLE - X Roads ½ mile South of second E of SOLERNEAU - main DOULLENS - ARRAS Road to LE BAC DU SUD - BAILLEULVAL - BASSEUX - BELLACOURT - BRETENCOURT.

6. SUPPLIES --
   Refilling Point for Supplies on 30th - LA BELLEVUE 9.0 a.m.

7. MARCH DISCIPLINE --

   A distance of 500 yards will be maintained between each Section.

8. AMMUNITION --

   Echelons will move empty.

9. BILLETS --
   All billets must be left clean and in a sanitary condition before departure.

10. A C K N O W L E D G E.

                                           Dean   2nd Lieut.
                           for Adjutant 50th Divnal Amman Column.

    Issued at   p.m.

    Copy No 1.   1st Section.
     "   " 2.   2nd   "
     "   " 3.   'B' Echelon.
     "   " 4.   War Diary.
     "   " 5 & 6. Spare.

SECRET

ADDENDUM to OPERATION ORDER No 17 by Lieut Colonel F.W. CLUFF R.F.A. (T) Commanding 50th Divisional Ammunition Column.

1. 50th D. A. C. will now move to a position just east of MONCHIET instead of WAILLY.

2. ROUTE
   COULLEMONT - COUTURELLE - cross roads a quarter mile south of second E in SOLERNEAU - main DOULLENS - ARRAS road - LE BAC DU SUD.

J. Dean.
for Adjutant 50th Div: Amm: Column.   2Lieut

Army Form C. 2118.

WAR DIARY

50th DIVISIONAL AMMUNITION COLUMN

INTELLIGENCE SUMMARY.

(Erase heading not required.)

Page 1   VOLUME III   APRIL 1917.

Vol 2

Instructions regarding War Diaries and Intelligence Summaries are contained in F. S. Regs., Part II. and the Staff Manual respectively. Title pages will be prepared in manuscript.

Place	Date	Hour	Summary of Events and Information	Remarks and references to Appendices
MONCHIET	1-4-17		The unit sent a party to collect 120 remounts from BOULOGNE	
	4-4-17		40 Remounts were collected from PREVENT	
	7-4-17		25 Remounts were taken over to 251 Brigade R.F.A.	
			95 " " " " 250 Brigade R.F.A.	
	1st to 7/4/17		During this period a considerable amount of ammunition was delivered to batteries. Owing to the very severe weather many animals suffered acutely from exposure.	
	8-4-17		40 Remounts were collected from PREVENT. The unit attached 228 mules from "B" Echelon to the Infantry Brigades (76 per Bde) for pack work in connexion with the recent fighting. The limbered portion of the S.A.A. section was attached to Div. Hd. Qrs. Owing to the unit supplying pack animals to Inf. Bdes, and L.D. horses to Artillery Brigades	

Army Form C. 2118.

WAR DIARY
INTELLIGENCE SUMMARY.

50TH DIVISIONAL AMMUNITION COLUMN

Page IV

(Erase heading not required.)

Place	Date	Hour	Summary of Events and Information	Remarks and references to Appendices
	9.4.17 10.4.17 13.4.17		It became as a Mobile ammobile. With the remaining animals and personnel the 1st Section of H.T. Echelon was made mobile.	
	14.4.17 17.4.17		A party proceeded to BOULOGNE to collect 50 rounds Nothing of importance beyond ordinary routine work	
			A party proceeded to BOULOGNE to collect 81 rounds from 6 H Jue and H.T.R Section joined the unit from B/250 and D/250 Brigades respectively. The mobile section proceeded to forward wagon lines at G.26.a Sheet 51.B 1:40,000.	Greaten dated No. 18 attached
	18.4.17 20.4.17 21.4.17		The mobile section of the unit delivered ammunition to the batteries. 14 remounts were handed over to Infantry Brigades HQ L.D. Horses were handed over to 250 Brigade R.F.A. a/o 77/592 Pt Murray W. awarded "Military Medal".	

1577 Wt.W10791/1773 500,000 1/15 D.D.&L. A.D.S.S./Forms/C. 2118.

Army Form C. 2118.

WAR DIARY

INTELLIGENCE SUMMARY.

50th DIVISIONAL AMMUNITION COLUMN

Page III

(Erase heading not required.)

Instructions regarding War Diaries and Intelligence Summaries are contained in F. S. Regs., Part II. and the Staff Manual respectively. Title pages will be prepared in manuscript.

Place	Date	Hour	Summary of Events and Information	Remarks and references to Appendices
	23.4.17 24.4.17 26.4.17		24 L.D mules were collected from TREVANT. 27 L.D horses were handed over to 250 Brigade R.F.A. The limbered portion of the S.A.A section reformed the unit from Div. H.Q. The pack animals rejoined the unit from Infantry Brigades.	
	26th to 27.4.17 29.4.17		The Gun portion of the 2nd Section of "B" Echelon was found by "B" Echelon & proceeded to L 26 a sheet 51B 1:40,000 to assist in delivery of ammunition to Batteries. The condition of the camp on occupation by this unit was in a very insanitary condition. The camp has since been rendered sanitary by the cutting of drains, the erection of ablution benches, and the re-sitting of cook houses and latrines	Operation order 4/17 /9 attached

H. Cruft
Lieut Colonel

Copy No. 5

ADDENDUM TO OPERATION ORDER NO. 20 BY
LIEUT COL L. C. DRURY., R.A., COMMANDING,
50th Divisional Ammunition Column.

Relief of 'B' Echelon by No 2 Section.

No 2 Section will move off from
MONCHIET at 8.30 a.m. tomorrow, the 17th
instant.

D Hay
Captain.
Adjutant 50th D. A. C.

16.5.17.

Copy No 1.   1st Section.
Copy No 2.   2nd Section.
Copy No 3.   'B' Echelon.
Copy No 4.   War Diary.
Copy No 5 & 6.   Spare.

Copy No. 6.

OPERATION ORDERS No 20 BY LIEUT COL H.C. DRURY., R.A.
COMMANDING 50th DIVISIONAL AMMUNITION COLUMN.

1. No 2 Section will relieve the 'B' Echelon at ARRAS during the 16th and 17th May, 1917.

2. On 16th instant, O.C. No 1 Section will send 56 L.D. horses to Brigades from his own L.D. and those attached to him from No 2 Section. 28 L.D. will be handed over to 250 Brigade and 28 to 251 Brigade. Receipts will be taken for horses and remount hand-collars.

3. On same day, 16th instant, Lieut HILLYARD and remaining 2nd Section animals attached to No 1 Section, will be attached to 'B' Echelon. Lieut HILLYARD will take :-
   Riders.   Pr L.D.   Mules.   Total .
   9   1   36   46

4. On same day 16th instant, O.C. 'B' Echelon will transfer to No 1 Section :-
   Riders.   L.D.   Mules.   Total .
   6   ---   69   75.

No 1 Section will then be complete to establishment .

5. On the 17th instant, No 2 section will march to ARRAS and take over from 'B' Echelon. All 2nd Section wagons, and S.A.A. Section will be taken over.
O.C. 'B' Echelon will transfer to No 2 Section the following animals :-   Riders.   L.D.   Mules.   Total .
                                 6   ---   157   163.
On relief O.C. 'B' Echelon will march back to MONCHIET.
O.C. Sections will arrange loan of teams for moving .

6. O.C. No 2 Section will transfer 10 L.D. horses selected by O.C. to No 1 Section. O.C. No 1 Section will also transfer 4 L.D. debility horses to O.C. 'B' Echelon .

7. O.C. 'B' Echelon will take back to MONCHIET 4 L.D. horses from No 1 Section and in addition to his remaining animals. He will on arrival at MONCHIET take over the following sick and als left behind by No 2 Section :-
   Riders.   L.D.   Mules.   Total .
   1   16   10   27.

8. All animals transferred between Sections will be immediately taken on or off the strength of the Section to which they are transferred.

9. The following officers will be attached temporarily to No 2 Section :-   Lieut GEYPEL .
                                 2nd Lieut RAWLINSON .
                                 2nd Lieut WEBSTER .

10.   Ration Indents will be changed to-day 16th instant to the new strengths.
        Interim adjustments will be arranged by B.Q.M.S. GIBSON in conjunction with Section B.Q.M.Ss.

11.   O.C. No 1 Section will send with **56** L.D. Remounts to Brigades to-day, forage for consumption on 16th and 17th.   He will send rations for 18th and 19th at a subsequent date.

        O.C. No 1 Section will strike these remounts off his A.B. 55 ~~tomorrow morning~~ 16th instant

12.   O.C. 'B' Echelon will temporarily attach the following drivers to 'A' Echelon.
            To No 1 Section .   40 .
            To No 2 Section .   20 .
                                        ----
                                        60 .

13.   All wagons will be taken over by the Sections to which they belong.

14.   Section Commanders will report completion by 9 a.m. 18th instant and will render a Statement showing :-

        (1) Actual effective strength of personnel & animals.
        (2)   Do.   Ration   "   "   "   "
        (3) Detail Statement of personnel and animals attached.
        (4)   "   "   "   "   "   "   dettached

in addition to the A.F.B. 213 which will reach this office by 12 (noon) on 18.5.17.

                        Captain.
                Adjutant 50th Divisional Ammunition Column.

16.5.17.

    Copy No 1.   O.C. No 1 Section.
     "   " 2.   "   " 2   "
     "   " 3.   "   " 'B' Echelon.
     "   " 4.   The Diary.
     "   " 5 &
            6   Spare.

SECRET.   Copy No. 1.

OPERATION ORDER NO 18 BY LIEUT COL F.W. CLUFF., R.F.A.(T).
Commanding 50th Divisional Ammunition Column.
----

1. No 1 Section, 50th Divisional Ammunition Column will move this afternoon as soon as possible to new Lines, G.26.a. Sheet 51 B, 1/40,000

2. The following transport will be taken :-
   - 18   18-pdr Wagons .
   - 6   4.5" Howr Wagons .
   - 8   G.S. Wagons for S.A.A.
   - 4   G.S. Wagons for Bridges .
   - 2   "   "   " Grenades .
   - 1   "   "   " Technical Stores .
   - 1   Water Cart

3. All sick men and horses will be handed over to O.C. No 2 Section .

4. TRANSPORT

   O.C. No 2 Section will lend to No 1 Section 5 G.S. Wagons loaded with the normal complement of S.A.A.

5. The following additional teams and men will be loaned from 'B' Echelon, 4 Teams, complete with harness and drivers .
                                                20 Other Ranks .
   " 2nd Section   2 Teams, complete with harness and drivers .

   ONE days rations and forage will be handed over to No 1 Section for the above AT ONCE.

6. On arrival in the new area, a mounted orderly (cyclist if possible) will be attached to D.A.H.Q.

7. On arrival at the new area , four G.S. Wagons will be kept empty by dumping the loads in order to supply any fatigues that may be ordered .

8. The orderly from these Headquarters to D.A.H.Q. will call at the 1st Section Lines daily at 9.30 a.m. and 5.30 p.m.

9. ACKNOWLEDGE.

                                        D. Hay
                                        Captain.
                            Adjutant 50th Divisional Ammunition Column.

Issued at   p.m. 17.4.17.

Copy No 1.   War Diary .
 "   " 2.   1st Section.
 "   " 3.   2nd   "
 "   " 4.   'B' Echelon.
 "   " 5.   Spare .

SECRET.   Copy 1.

AMENDMENT TO OPERATION ORDER NO 18 By Lieut Col
F.W. CLUFF., R.F.A.(T)., Cmdg 50th D.A.C.

Paragraphs 2 and 7 are amended as follows :-
These four wagons FOR BRIDGES will travel light and will be used for fatigues.

D Hay
Captain.
Adjutant 50th D.A.C.

Issued at   p.m. 17.4.17.

Copy No 1   War Diary.
"   "   2   1st Section.
"   "   3   2nd   "
"   "   4   'B' Echelon.
"   "   5   Spare.

SECRET.   Copy...1..

OPERATION ORDER NO 19 BY LIEUT COL F.W. CLUFF., R.F.A.(T).
COMMANDING 50TH DIVISIONAL AMMUNITION COLUMN.

1.   'B' Echelon will move at 8.30 a.m. tomorrow 29th
        instant to forward wagon lines at G.26.a. Sheet 51 B.

2.   No 2 Section will hand over 19 full ammunition wagons
        18-pdr and 4.5" Howr. The 5 18-pdr wagons now attached
        to No 1 Section will be handed over to 'B' Echelon.

3.   No 1 Section will hand over the 5 'B' Echelon
        teams with drivers and harness, on arrival of 'B' Echelon,
        and also the remaining 20 men at present attached to No 1
        Section ~~Section~~ (35 men in all).

4.   No 2 Section will attach to 'B' Echelon 6 limber
        gunners including an N.C.O. who will be responsible to
        O.C. 'B' Echelon for the wagons and stores.

5.   O.C. 'B' Echelon will have with him the following
        transport :-   24 limbered Ammunition Wagons.
                        1 G.S. Wagon .Technical Stores.
                        1   "   "   Grenades.
                        2   "   "   Cartridge Containers.
                        8   "   "   Empty.
                        ____
                Total 36
                        ____
                        1 Water Cart attached.

6.   REAR PARTY --
        7 Sick men will be left behind attached to No 2
        Section, also 2 N.C.Os. and 7 men for care of sick
        animals, harness and wagons - Total 2 N.C.Os. 14 Men.

7.   1/2 Riders and 30 Mules sick will be left behind
        in charge of O.C. No 2 Section and shewn as attached to him.

8.   Harness & Wagons --   O.C.'B' Echelon will leave
        behind 8 team sets of harness complete and also a quantity
        of spare harness in his present harness hut, also 2 G.S.
        Wagons   O.C. No 2 Section will arrange for 'B' Echelon
        light duty men to work on the harness and to make good
        deficiencies.   Receipts to be given for wagons and
        harness left behind.

9.   O.C. No 2 Section will return 15 men of the 1st
        Section at present attached to him to No 1 Section.

10.   Sergt Baxter and 7 No 1 Section drivers will
        tomorrow morning rejoin No 1 Section with the 7 S.A.A.
        Carts, and also the 2 drivers and 4 mules now attached
        to 'B' Echelon (returned from pack work). Two days
        rations and forage will be taken.

11.   On arrival in new area O.C.'B' Echelon will report to Staff Captain 50th D.A. 'B' Echelon will be required to supply ammunition to 250 Brigade.

12.   A.S.C. have been advised of move of 'B' Echelon. O.C. Sections will mutually adjust rations and forage where necessary.

13.   The 25 No 2 Section teams at present attached to No 1 Section will remain so attached.

14.   The various transfers of men and animals mentioned above, will be carefully shown by Section Commanders in their Daily Parade States rendered to this Office.

15.   A C K N O W L E D G E .

D Hay

Captain.
Adjutant 50th Divisional Ammunition Column.

28.4.17.   Issued at   ...... p.m.

Copy No 1.   War Diary.
"   " 2.   1st Section.
"   " 3.   2nd Section.
"   " 4.   'B' Echelon.
"   " 5 & 6.   Spare.

Army Form C. 2118.

WAR DIARY
or
INTELLIGENCE SUMMARY.
(Erase heading not required.)

VOLUME No 26.

50TH DIVISIONAL AMMUNITION COLUMN

May 1917

Vol 22

Place	Date	Hour	Summary of Events and Information	Remarks and references to Appendices
MONCHIET	May 8th		Nothing to record beyond ordinary routine work. Collected 102 remounts from TREVANT.	
	9th & 14th		Lt Col. F.W. CLUFF R.F.A. (T) relinquished command of the unit on transfer to ENGLAND at midnight 8th to 9th May 1917. Lt Col. R.C. DRURY R.F.A took over command of the unit at midnight 8th to 9th May 1917, from 286 Bde. R.F.A. Ordinary routine work.	
	15th & 16th		2 Riders and 144 L.D horses were sent to Hartley Brigades. The unit was reorganised in order to complete the "A" Echelon.	
	17th		The 2nd Section of the "A" Echelon proceeded to ARRAS in relief of "B" Echelon, who returned to MONCHIET	Operation Order No 20 attached

Army Form C. 2118.

VOLUME No 26 WAR DIARY or INTELLIGENCE SUMMARY. 50th DIVISIONAL AMMUNITION COLUMN

(Erase heading not required.)

Place	Date	Hour	Summary of Events and Information	Remarks and references to Appendices
	May			
	19th		To L.D. Mules were collected from AUBIGNY.	
	20th			
	21st			
	22nd			
	23rd		Nothing beyond ordinary routine work. The following W.O.'s have been mentioned in despatches for gallantry and devotion to duty in the Field. No. 9662 B.S.M. H.O. WITHERS No. 10000 B.S.M. R.P. KIRKUP The "A" Echelon moved from M.26.D to M.13.D. Sheet 51 B. Ordinary routine work.	
	25th			
	26th		The "A" Echelon moved from M.13.D to M.16.D. Sheet 51 D.	
	29th		During the move a great amount of instruction was given to Officers & men fusing and refitting reinforcements from the Base fitting them for work in the battle.	
	29th			

R.C. Drury
Lt. Col. R.A.
Commanding 50th Divisional Ammunition Column.

WAR DIARY

INTELLIGENCE SUMMARY

151st DIVISIONAL AMMUNITION COLUMN

VOLUME XXVII   Vol 23   JUNE 1917

Army Form C. 2118.

Place	Date	Hour	Summary of Events and Information	Remarks and references to Appendices
BEAUMAINS	JUNE 1st-3rd		Riding & report beyond ordinary routine work.	
"	14th		Collected 30 L.D. horses and 72 L.D. mules from SAULTY – L'ARBRET and handed over to 250 B'de R.F.A. 10 L.D. horses and to 251 B'de R.F.A. 20 L.D. horses	
"	5th 6th 16th		Nothing to report beyond ordinary routine work.	
"	"		Sent party to collect 5 Riding 80 L.D. horses and 20 L.D. mules from ABBEVILLE	
"	17th		The Head Quarters and "B" Echelon moved to forward wagon lines at M.17.C.78. that 51.B.	Operation Order No 21 attached
"	18th		Got over H.R.T. from 14th Div.	
"	21st		2 Riding and 42 L.D. horses handed over to 250 Bde. R.F.A. 2 Riding and 38 L.D. horses handed over to 251 Bde. R.F.A.	
"	22nd to 30th		Nothing to report beyond ordinary routine work.	
"			On the 27th the enemy shelled the vicinity of the 2nd Section, resulting in No 770256 Bdr Hoban T.J. and No 770474	

Army Form C. 2118.

WAR DIARY

~~INTELLIGENCE~~ SUMMARY

50TH DIVISIONAL AMMUNITION COLUMN

(Erase heading not required.)

Place	Date	Hour	Summary of Events and Information	Remarks and references to Appendices
			Dr Jones & being killed, and No 771955 Dr Jones J. Evans being wounded. Owing to the congestion of wagon lines in this area the 2nd Section moved to N.29.a.08 sheet 51.B. Since the H.Qrs + "B" echelon moved forward much work has been done in tack away, a number of G.S. wagons being detailed daily for the carrying of stone for the repair of roads. A great amount of ammunition has been salved from vacated gun positions.	

HGallagher.
Capt. R.F.A.
Commanding 50th Divisional Ammunition Column.

Secret.   Copy No ...1...

OPERATION ORDER NO 21 BY LIEUT COL R. C. DRURY., R.A.
COMMANDING 50th DIVISIONAL AMMUNITION COLUMN.

1.   Headquarters and 'B' Echelon will move to Forward Area at about M.16.c., Sheet 51 B on Sunday 17th instant.

2.   Headquarters will leave MONCHIET Camp at 9 a.m.
       'B' Echelon   "   "   "   "   " 9.15 a.m.

3.   O.C. No 1 and 2 Sections will each send to Headquarters on the afternoon of the 16th instant three empty G.S. Wagons (C.T.Os) (1 N.C.O. per Section) to assist in removal of surplus stores. 24 hours feeds and rations to be carried. Teams and wagons will remain over-night and move with H.Q.

4.   D.T.M.O. will lend 'B' Echelon 50 men from 9 a.m. to 12 (mid-day) the 16th instant, to assist in loading up.

5.   O.C. 'B' Echelon will leave a rear cleaning up party under an Officer to clear up lines and huts and guard wagons left behind. This party will march to Forward Area afternoon of 17th instant with wagons detailed in para (6). Certificate to be rendered to H.Q. on arrival as to condition Camp is left in.

6.   O.C. No 1 and 2 Sections will _each_ send 8 skeleton teams under an officer to report to Officer in Charge 'B' Echelon Rear Party at 10 a.m. on 17th instant. These teams will hook into 16 'B' Echelon wagons left behind and bring to Forward Area the same afternoon.

7.   A C K N O W L E D G E.

                                                     Captain.
                                        Adjutant 50th D. A. C.

Issued at   a.m. 16.6.17.

War Diary.   Copy No 1.
1st Section.   "   " 2.
2nd   "   "   " 3.
'B' Echelon.   "   " 4.
Spare.   "   " 5.

Secret.

Copy ..1..

AMENDMENTS TO OPERATION ORDER NO 21 BY LIEUT COL R.C. DRURY.,
COMMANDING 50th DIVISIONAL AMMUNITION COLUMN.

Amendment :-

Para 6 is cancelled and the following substituted :-

(a) O.C. No 1 Section will send 5 skeleton teams to assist in removal of 'B' Echelon Wagons.

(b) O.C. No 1 Section will also send 3 G.S.Wagons(C.T.Os.) to assist in removal of timber etc. These teams to report to Gnr HILLAM., H.Q.S.

(c) O.C. No 2 Section will send 5 skeleton teams to assist in removal of 'B' Echelon wagons.

(d) O.C. No 2 Section will send 3 G.S.Wagons(C.T.Os) to collect 114,000 rounds S.A.A. on 2nd Section charge. The above are in addition to wagons detailed under (3). An officer will be i/c each section party. Teams and wagons to leave at 6 a.m. on 17th instant.

Add to Para (5).

Officer i/c Rear Party will before leaving obtain a certificate from Town Major, MONCHIET, that camp has been left in a clean and sanitary condition.

Add.

O.C. 'B' Echelon will detail One G.S. Wagon with 6 mules to report to D.A. Headquarters, BEAUMETZ, 17th instant, at 2.15 p.m. to take load to new Headquarters at S.17.a. Sheet 51 B.
After unloading this wagon will proceed to new lines.

Captain.
Adjutant 50th D. A. C.

Issued at   p.m. 16.6.17.
Copy No 1.   War Diary.
"   " 2.   1st Section.
"   " 3.   2nd   "
"   " 4.   'B' Echelon.
"   " 5.   Spare.

Note. If teams detailed above under (a) & (c) have already left, they will be accommodated overnight at MONCHIET and will proceed at 9.15am 17th inst with 'B' Echelon.

Army Form C. 2118.

WAR DIARY
INTELLIGENCE SUMMARY.
50th DIVISIONAL AMMUNITION COLUMN

(Erase heading not required.) PAGE I VOLUME XXVIII July 1917

24

Place	Date	Hour	Summary of Events and Information	Remarks and references to Appendices
BEAURAINS	July 1st to 10		Nothing to report beyond ordinary routine work.	
	11th to 12th		Collected 34 LD mules from BEAUMETZ. Ordinary routine work.	
	17th		Collected 15 LD horses from BEAUMETZ	
	17th		Collected 20 Ride 20 LD horses and 44 LD mules from FREVENT	
	18th		12 LD horses handed over to 250 Bris+BE R.F.A.	
	19th		2 Ride and 5 LD horses handed over to 251 Bde. R.F.A.	
	20th to 26th		Nothing to report beyond ordinary routine work	
	24th		No. 386143 Pte Watson H. R.A.M.C. T/at (Nav) Field Ambulance attached to this unit awarded Military Medal, for attending wounded under shell fire.	
	27th		Commenced work on mould standings for horses at ST a sheet 51.B. on FICHEUX — BOIRY ST. RICTRUDE road.	

Army Form C. 2118.

WAR DIARY

INTELLIGENCE SUMMARY. 50TH DIVISIONAL AMMUNITION COLUMN

(Erase heading not required.) Page VI

Instructions regarding War Diaries and Intelligence Summaries are contained in F. S. Regs., Part II. and the Staff Manual respectively. Title pages will be prepared in manuscript.

Place	Date	Hour	Summary of Events and Information	Remarks and references to Appendices
	July 28th & 31st		Nothing to report beyond ordinary routine work. During the week the salvage of ammunition continued. A number of G.S. waggons have been detailed daily for the carting of stone to repair roads in the back area.	

Redmond
Lieut Col
Commanding 50th Divisional Ammunition Column

Army Form C. 2118.

WAR DIARY 50th DIVISIONAL AMMUNITION COLUMN

INTELLIGENCE SUMMARY.

VOLUME XXIX Page I AUGUST 1917

Vol 25

Place	Date	Hour	Summary of Events and Information	Remarks and references to Appendices
BEAURAINS	Aug 1	-	Nothing to report	
"	6.6	-	Ammunition commenced to be issued from A.R.P (No 11)	
"	Aug 6 to 26	-	General Routine work. Various fatigues including a good many to front line during which 5 men + a number of mules were wounded.	
"	Aug 28	-	Unit again reorganised. B Echelon converted into an S.A.A Section with 4 mule teams. Gun ammunition only. carried by No 1 & 2 Sections which are now practically Brigade Columns in constitution. Strength of unit now reduced by 91 men, 155 animals, 418 G.S Wagons. Headquarters slightly increased in strength	
	Aug 31		B Echelon moved to FICHEUX takes over the sole duty of work on winter standings.	

Repairing
Lieut. Colonel
Comdg 50th Divl Amm Column

CONFIDENTIAL.

WAR DIARY

OF

50TH DIVISIONAL AMMUNITION COLUMN.

from 1st September, 1917 to 30th September, 1917.

VOLUME No 30.

WAR DIARY
-or-
INTELLIGENCE SUMMARY

Army Form C. 2118.

50th DIVISIONAL AMMUNITION COLUMN

Place	Date	Hour	Summary of Events and Information	Remarks and references to Appendices
BEAURAINS	Sept 1/3		Nothing to report.	
	Sept 4		2nd Section moved to X.6.c Sheet 51.c to assist in carrying out the work on winter standings.	Serial Order No 22 attached
	Sept 7/23		16 additional G.S. Waggons on loan from 50th Divnl Train reported to speed up the work on winter standings. 1st Section moved to X.6.c Sheet 51.c for work in conjunction with winter standings.	Serial order No 23 attached
FICHEUX	Sept 24/30		H.Qrs. 50th D.A.C. moved to 37.B.24. During the month every effort has been made to push on the work on Winter Standings.	Serial order No 24 attached

R.C.Bruny
Lieut Col.
Commanding 50th D.A.C.

SECRET.   Copy No. 5.

Operation Orders No 22 by Lieut Colonel R. C. DRURY., R.A.
Commanding 50th Divisional Ammunition Column.
───────────────────────────────

1.   No 2 Section will move to X.6.c. Sheet 51.c. forthwith
in order to carry out work on Winter Standings.

        Move to be completed by 5th inst.

2.   Limbered Ammunition Wagons will, before moving,
be handed over to O.C. No 1 Section who will arrange to
guard the wagons by night.   Limber Gunners will be left
with wagons to continue overhauling etc.

3.   O.C. No 1 Section will supply two wagons nightly
for 181 Tunnelling Coy. R.E. commencing 4th inst.   No 2 Section
will lend No 1 Section 2 G.S. Wagons to enable them to do
this.

4.   Teams for 151 Infantry Brigade.
        The 4 teams that are being daily supplied to 151
Infantry Brigade by No 2 Section will, commencing tomorrow,
be found by No 1 Section.
        O.C. No 2 Section will inform O.C. No 1 Section of
the daily arrangements for these wagons, and will put him
in a position to carry on to-morrow.

5.   Teams and Wagons at D.T.M.O.
        The three 2nd section teams will be relieved forthwith
by three No 1 Section teams.   The three 2nd Section, G.S.
Wagons will remain there, but will be taken on charge by No
1 Section, receipts being given.

        No 1 Section will supply a N.C.O. to relieve the
2nd Section N.C.O.

        Mutual adjustment of forage and rations to be made.

                                        Day
                                        Captain.
                        Adjutant, 50th Divisional Ammunition Column

Timed 2.15.pm 4.9.17.

        Copy No 1,   War Diary.
         "   " 2, No 1 Section.
         "   " 3,   " 2   "
         "   " 4, S.A.A. Section.
         "   " 5, Spare
         "   " 6, Spare.

SECRET.   Copy. No. 1.

Operation Orders No 23 by LIEUT COLONEL R.C. DRURY., R.A.
Commanding 50th Divisional Ammunition Column.
---

1. No: 1 Section will move to X.6.c., Sheet 51 C. forthwith.
    Move to be completed by 20th inst.

2. Certificate to be rendered to this office by 6 pm 21st
    to the effect that the camp was left in a clean and
    sanitary condition.

3. WATER AND RATIONS FOR A. R. P.
    O.C. No 1 Section will continue to ration the whole of
    personnel detached from the unit to A.R.P. up to and
    including rations for consumption on 21.9.17. From the
    22.9.17 and onwards, A. R. P. personnel will be rationed
    by 23rd B. A. C.
    O.C. No 1 section will supply A.R.P. with water for
    consumption on 18.9.17, after which date water will be
    supplied by 23rd B.A.C.

4. ACKNOWLEDGE

                                    [signature] Captain,
                        Adjutant 50th Divisional Ammunition Column.

Issued at 10.30 am 18.9.17.

Copy No 1.   War Diary.
  " No 2.   No 1 Section.
  " No 3.   No 2 Section.
  " No 4.   SAA. Section.
  " No 5.   23rd B.A.C.
  " No 6.   Spare.

SECRET   Copy No: 1.

OPERATION ORDER NO 24 by Lieut Colonel R.C.DRURY., R.A.
           Commanding 50th Divisional Ammunition Column.
---

1. Headquarters, 50th D. A. C. will move from M.22.c.78.
    Sheet 51.B. to S.7.B.24. Sheet 51.B. on 20.9.17.

2. Headquarters Office will close at M.22.c.78 at 10 am
    and re-open at 10 am 20.9.17 at S.7.a.24. Sheet.51.B.

3. ACKNOWLEDGE.

                        Dean   2nd Lieut
               for Adjutant 50th Divisional Ammunition Column.

Issued at 10.45 am 19.9.17.

Copy No 1. War Diary.
 "   No 2. Staff Captain 50th D.A.
 "   No 3. No 1 Section.
 "   No 4. No 2 Section.
 "   No 5. SAA. Section.
 "   No 6. No 11 A.R.P.
 "   No 7. Spare.

Army Form C. 2118.

WAR DIARY 50TH DIVISIONAL AMMUNITION COLUMN.

INTELLIGENCE SUMMARY.

(Erase heading not required.)

VOLUME XXXI   OCTOBER 1917

SHEET N° 1

Instructions regarding War Diaries and Intelligence Summaries are contained in F. S. Regs., Part II. and the Staff Manual respectively. Title pages will be prepared in manuscript.

Place	Date	Hour	Summary of Events and Information	Remarks and references to Appendices
FICHEUX	Oct. 1st to 21st		Nothing to report beyond work on winter standings for the Divisional Artillery.	
	21st & 22nd		1st Section entrained at GOUY and detrained at PESLEHOEK. 4 limbered Ammunition Wagons, 1 G.S. Wagon, mules and personnel proceeded with each Battery of the 251 Brigade RFA. Remainder of the Section proceeded with H.Q. 251 Brigade RFA.	Operation Order No 25 attached
			2nd Section entrained at BEAUMETZ and detrained at PROVEN. 4 limbered Ammunition Wagons, 1 G.S. Wagon, mules and personnel proceeded with each Battery of the 250 Brigade RFA. Remainder of the Section proceeded with H.Q. 250 Brigade RFA.	
	22nd		H.Q. D.A.C. entrained at BEAUMETZ with N°1 Coy 50th Divisional Train and detrained at PROVEN.	

SHEET No 2

WAR DIARY 50TH DIVISION

INTELLIGENCE SUMMARY.

Place	Date	Hour	Summary of Events and Information
	Oct. 22nd		½ S.A.A. Section entrained at GOUY with ½ D.T. Mortar Brigade and detrained at PESELHOEK.
			½ S.A.A. Section entrained at BEAUMETZ with ½ D.T. Mortar Brigade and detrained at PROVEN.
			On detraining the Unit marched direct to the following places:- Headquarters and 'A' Echelon. B.16.a. Sheet 28. S.A.A. Section. B.21.c. Sheet 28.
			The move was completed on 23rd October, 1917.
ELVERDINGHE.	24th		The 'A' Echelon commenced delivery of ammunition to batteries and continued to the end of the month supplying as much as possible. All deliveries were by pack animals.

SHEET No 3

Army Form C. 2118.

WAR DIARY 50TH DIVISIONAL AMMUNITION COLUMN

INTELLIGENCE SUMMARY

(Erase heading not required.)

Place	Date	Hour	Summary of Events and Information	Remarks and references to Appendices
ELVERDINGHE	Oct. 29.		An Ammunition Dump was started at D 10 d 5.4 Sheet 28 to facilitate delivery of ammunition. The dump being supplied direct from railhead LUNAVILLE, B.16.88 sheet 28 by lorry and by our own G.S. Wagons. Immediately on arrival in the new area the S.A.A. Section were placed under the orders of "Q" Branch for work in connection with infantry. RCDrury Lieut Colonel Commanding 50th Divisional Ammunition Column.	

Confidential.

WAR DIARY

OF

50TH DIVISIONAL AMMUNITION COLUMN.

FROM 1.11.17. TO 30.11.17.

VOLUME NO XXXII.

SHEET. No. 1

Army Form C. 2118.

WAR DIARY
of 50th DIVISIONAL AMMUNITION COLUMN
~~INTELLIGENCE SUMMARY.~~
(Erase heading not required.)

Place	Date	Hour	Summary of Events and Information	Remarks and references to Appendices
ILVERDINGHE	1917 Nov 8			
	9th		Nothing to report beyond ordinary routine work. Ammunition dump at B.10.d.54 sheet 28 was closed and LICHTFIELD Dump at B.15.d.94 was taken over.	
	10th		On the division vacating this area the S.A.A. section came under the orders of "Q" Branch of the 17th Div for work in connection with infantry.	
	15th		No. 775141 Cpl Kelley W. awarded "Military Medal" for Gallantry under shell fire.	
	16th		Salvage work commenced in the area of the Right Artillery Group Canal between C.19.a.21 and B.12.b.66 and NE to V.29.a.9 and up 32.d.39 & sheet 20 of sheet 25 also NE to V.29.a.9 and Nothing to report beyond ordinary routine work.	
	17th 26			
	27th		The following N.C.O's — awarded Military Medals for Gallantry in the Field. No. 771523 Sgt Jackson J.J. No. 75508+2 Cpl Littlewood C. No. 53786 Bdr Kynvery A.B.	

1577 Wt.W10791/1773 500,000 1/15 D.D.&L. A.D.S.S./Forms/C. 2118.

SHEET No 2.
Army Form C. 2118.

WAR DIARY 50th DIVISIONAL AMMUNITION COLUMN

INTELLIGENCE SUMMARY.

Place	Date	Hour	Summary of Events and Information	Remarks and references to Appendices
EVERDINGHE	Febr 1917		During the month the work in connection with the construction of horse standings and shelters was renewed.	

A.M.Stephen. Capt. R.F.A.
Commanding 50th D.A.C.

Operation No 28 (Part ii).

Relief Table.

Unit.	Location.	Relieving Unit.	Time of Relief To be clear of camp by.
XXX.			
No 1 Section 39 D.A.C.	G.4.d.31.	No 1 Section 50 D.A.C.	11 a.m.
No 2 Section 39 D.A.C.	G.10.b.18.	SAA Section 50 D.A.C.	11.30 a.m.
SAA Section 39 D.A.C.	G.10.a.78.	No 2 Section 50 D.A.C.	12 noon.

Army Form.

WAR DIARY

Lt. Col. Comm. Col. ~~or~~
INTELLIGENCE SUMMARY.

50 Divisional Ammunition Column

(Erase heading not required.) Volume XXIII DECEMBER 1917

Instructions regarding War Diaries and Intelligence Summaries are contained in F.S. Regs., Part II. and the Staff Manual respectively. Title pages will be prepared in manuscript.

Vol 29

Place	Date	Hour	Summary of Events and Information	Remarks and references to Appendices
VLAMER-TINGHE	1st to 10		Nothing beyond Routine work to report —	
	15		Nos 1 + 2 sections moved to Camp at G.15.a (Sheet 28)	Op. Order No 26 Battery No 27 attached
			HQ: SD DAC + SAA moved to Camp at G.9.c — do —	
	21		VIII Corps Gun Pool taken over from 39 D.A.C	
			"B" Amm'n Dump taken over from 39 D.A.C	
			Salvage work taken over from 39 D.A.C	
	22		50th D.A.C relieved 39 D.A.C	Op. Order No 28 attached
	24		S.A.A section moved to Camp H.16.a.4.4.	
	27		No 1 section moved to Camp H.15.a.2.1	
	28		HQ 50 DAC moved to Camp H.15.a.4.1.	

R.O. Murray Lt Colonel
Comdg 50 DAC

Secret.   Copy. No 4

Operation No 26 by Lt Col R.C. Drury., R.F.A.
Commanding 50th Divisional Amon Column.
_____

1. 1st and 2nd Sections, 50th D.A.C. will move
to G.15.a., Sheet 28 on 10.12.17.
   O.C. No 2 Section will march out of Camp
at 9.15 a.m.
   O.C. No 1 Section will march out of camp at
10 a.m.

2. REFILLING POINT --- Rations for consumption on
12th instant will be drawn from Corps Troops
Supply Column -- Refilling Point, L.12.a.28,
Sheet 27 at 8 a.m. 11th instant.

3. Camps will be handed over to Area Commandant
Bde Boesinghe Area No 2 tomorrow morning. Receipts
will be obtained for area stores and one copy
will be handed to Area Commandant and the other
forwarded to this office.
   A rear party of 1 Officer, 1 N.C.O. and 3 men
will be left behind to clean up camp, and act
as guard until handed over.

4. A c k n o w l e d g e.
                                    Captain.
                              Adjutant 50th D.A.C.
Issued at 10.15 p.m. 9.12.17.

Copy No 1.   1st Section.   Copy No 2   2nd Section
  " No 3.   SAA Section.   "   " 4 War Diary.
  " Nos 5 & 6. Spare.

SECRET   Copy No. 1.

OPERATION ORDER No 27 by Lieut Colonel R.C. DRURY. R.F.A.
Commanding 50th Divisional Ammunition Column.
----

1. Headquarters and S.A.A. Section 50th D.A.C. will
   move to G.9.c. Sheet 28 on 15th inst.
   Headquarters will be clear of ELVERDINGHE by 8.30 am
   SAA Section will be clear of ELVERDINGHE by 8.45 am.

2. Route :- ELVERDINGHE - POPERINGHE ROAD - SWITCH ROAD.

3. Camps will be handed over to Area Commandant or his
   representative. Receipts will be obtained for Area
   stores in duplicate, one copy will be handed to
   Area Commandant or his representative, the other
   forwarded to this Office.
   A certificate will also be obtained stating that the
   Camp was left in a clean and sanitary condition, and
   that the Nissen Huts were in good order.
   A rear party of One Officer and 3 other ranks will be
   left behind to clean up camps and act as guard until
   handed over.

                                                Captain.
                           Adjutant 50th Divisional Ammunition Column
Issued at 4.30 pm 14.12.17.

Copy No 1 War Diary.
 "   " 2 No 1 Section.
 "   " 3 xxx xxxxxxx No 2 Section.
 "   " 4 SAA Section.
 "   " 5 R.S.M.
 "   " 6 Spare.

SECRET.   Copy No 1.

OPERATION ORDERS No 28 (Part 1) by Lieut Colonel R.C.DRURY, RFA
Commanding 50th Divisional Ammunition Column.
----

1. In preparation for the relief of the 39th D.A.C. by the 50th
   D.A.C. on 22.12.17, the following reliefs will take place
   tomorrow 21.12.17 as follows :-
   (a) One officer and 15 other Ranks will relieve a similar party
       of 39th D.A.C. at the Ammunition Dump .I.5.a.49.
       O.C. No 1 Section will detail 1 Officer 1 Corporal (Corpl
       Jones) and 6 men.
       O.C. No 2 Section will detail 1 Bdr and 6 men.
       O.C. SAA Section will detail Dvr ROSE as clerk.
       This party will be rationed by O.C. No 1 Section who will
       also arrange to ration 45 men of a Labour Coy already at
       the dump.
       The relief will take place at 11.30 am.

   (b) O.C. No 2 Section will take over the VIII Corps Gun Park
       from 39th D.A.C. at 12 noon.
       He will detail 1 Officer 1 Bdr and 11 Other Ranks (one
       being a clerk) to take over the dump.
       He will detail wagons and teams as necessary.

   (c) 1 Officer and 12 Other ranks (including 2 N.C.Os and 1 Clerk)
       from No 1 Section with 4 G.S. Wagons C.T.Os will relieve
       a party from 39th D.A.C. at Salvage work and also a party
       constructing wagon lines east of the road running through
       I.3.b.   They will be rationed by No 1 Section.
       They will live in dug-outs, I.9.a.28 which will be handed
       over to them by the party relieved.
       The relief will be completed by 11.30 am.

2. Map Reference sheet 28.

3. Acknowledge.

                                                    Lieut
                            a/Adjutant 50th D. A. C.

Issued at 8.30 pm 20/12.17.

Copy No 1 War Diary
 "   No 2 No 1 Section.
 "   No 3 No 2 Section.
 "   No 4 SAA Section.
 "   No 5 R.S.M.
 "   No 6 Spare.

SECRET.   Copy No. 1.

OPERATION ORDERS No. 28 (Part ii) by Lieut Col R.C. Drury., R.F.A.
Commanding 59th Divisional Ammunition Column.

1. The 59th D.A.C. will relieve the 59th D.A.C. on the
   22nd instant as per relief table annexed.

2. Each Camp will be left in charge of a warden who will
   remain in the Camp till relieved.

   Forms of receipts in duplicate for all tents & huts on
   charge in each camp will be given to the warden.

   On relief the warden will obtain receipts in duplicate for
   everything handed over and forward one of the receipts to this
   office.

   Certificates will also be obtained that the camps have been
   left in a clean and sanitary condition and that the Nissen
   Huts are in good order.

   Section Commanders will ration their respective Camp
   Wardens till relieved.

3. Os.C. Sections will detail an officer and an advance
   party, to take over their respective camps, from the unit
   being relieved. They must arrive at the camps at 7 a.m.

4. Section Commanders will each detail a rear party of 3 men
   under a N.C.O. to complete the cleaning of their camps.

5. On arrival of the sections of the 53rd D.A.C. to take
   over the present camp an officer from each section will
   attend to get the necessary receipts and to hand over.
   The time of arrival will be notified later.

6. On completion of the relief, Section Commanders will at
   at once report in writing to H.Q. 59th D.A.C. that the relief
   is completed.

7. A c k n o w l e d g e.

                                                    Lieut.
                                          a/Adjutant 59th D.A.C.

Issued at 8.30 p.m. 21.12.17.

Copy No 1.   War Diary.   Copy No 4.   SAA Section.
Copy No 2.   1st Section.   Copy No 5.   R.S.M.
Copy No 3.   2nd Section.   Copy No 6.   Spare.

ADDENDUM ----   Officers detailed under para 3 will give no
                certificate as to cleanliness of the camps as the
                Area Commandant is being asked to inspect them.

CONFIDENTIAL.

WAR DIARY

of

50TH DIVISIONAL AMMUNITION COLUMN.

FROM 1.1.18 to 31.1.18.

VOLUME No: XXXIV.

PAGE 1   WAR DIARY 50TH DIVISIONAL AMMUNITION COLUMN (Army Form C. 2118.)

INTELLIGENCE SUMMARY.

(Erase heading not required.)

Instructions regarding War Diaries and Intelligence Summaries are contained in F. S. Regs., Part II. and the Staff Manual respectively. Title pages will be prepared in manuscript.

Place	Date	Hour	Summary of Events and Information	Remarks and references to Appendices
	1915			
VLAMERTINGHE	Jan 1 to Jan 7		Nothing to report beyond ordinary Routine Work.	
	9th		"B" Ammunition Dump (I.5a.49) personnel consisting of (1 Officer, 15 Other Ranks) relieved by 33rd DAC.	
			Sandridge Dump (I.5a.16) personnel consisting of (1 Officer, 9 Other Ranks) relieved by 33 DAC	
			Ammunition Salvage Party (I.36.9.b) — consisting of (1 Officer, 12 Other Ranks relieved by 33rd DAC.	
			Gun (60) handed over to 33rd DAC.	
POPERINGHE	9th		Headquarters, 1st and 2nd Section moved to wagon lines at G.15d (Sheet 28)	0029 attached
	10th		3rd Section moved to Wagon lines at G.15a (Sheet 28).	
OUDEZEELE	13th		Headquarters and Sections moved to OUDEZEELE	0030 attached
RENESCURE	14th		" " " " " RENESCURE.	0031 attached
MERCK ST LIEVIN	15th		" " " " " MERCK ST LIEVIN and No 1 Section to CLOQUANT and LA BUCAILLE	0032 attached

PAGE 2.

WAR DIARY 50TH DIVISIONAL AMMUNITION COLUMN.
INTELLIGENCE SUMMARY.

Place	Date	Hour	Summary of Events and Information	Remarks and references to Appendices
MERCK-ST-LIEVIN	Jan 16th to 26th		Resting	
	27th		Headquarters & Section DAC moved to CAMPAGNE AREA	0033 attached
	28th		do do moved to OUDEZEELE	O.O. 34 do
	29th		do do moved to POPERINGHE AREA	O.O. 35 attached
	31st		do do moved to VLAMERTINGHE AREA in relief of 33rd D.A.C.	in O.O. 36 attacks

ReSpmry
Lieut. Col.
Commanding 50th D.A.C.

Ref: Map HAZEBROUCK 5a 1/100.000.

SECRET COPY No. 1.

OPERATION ORDER NO 3# by Lieut Colonel R.C. DRURY, R.F.A.

Commanding 50th Divisional Ammunition Column.

---

1. The 50th Divisional Ammunition Column will march to OUDEZEELE on 28.1.18.

2. Order of march.
   Headquarters
   No 1 Section
   SAA Section.
   No 2 Section.

3. STARTING POINT: - On CAMPAGNE-OUDEZEELE road 200 yards West of RENESCURE CHURCH.
   Headquarters and the remainder of the Column will be closed up at the proper distances between Sections in the above order of march by 8.40 am.

4. ROUTE :- ZUYTPEENE - WEMAERS CAPPEL - OUDEZEELE.

5. Billets :- All billets will be left clean and a certificate to this effect will be handed in to this Headquarters 8.45 am

6. Baggage wagons will travel with their respective Sections.

7. Attention is called to D.A.Q.O. No 111 dated 25.1.18.

8. ACKNOWLEDGE.

Captain.
Adjutant 50th Divl Amm Column.

Issued at 5.10 pm 27.1.18.

Copy No 1 to War Diary.
Copy No 2 to No 1 Section.
Copy No 3 to No 2 Section.
Copy No 4 to SAA Section.
Copy No 5 to R.S.M.
Copy No 6 to Spare.
Copy No 7   Spare.

Copy No/...

SECRET   Ref: Map HAZEBROUCK 5a 1/100.000.

OPERATION ORDER No 35 by Lieut Colonel R.C.DRURY.R.F.A.
Commanding 50th Divisional Ammunition Column.
------------------@@------------------

1. The 50th D. A. C. will march to POPERINGHE - Area on 29.1.18.

2. Order of March :-
         Headquarters
         No 2 Section.
         No 1 Section.
         SAA Section.

3. Starting Point :- "T" roads 200 yards north of "D" in OUDEZEELE. Head of Headquarters will be at Starting Point with No 2 Section closed up at 8.45 am.
Head of No 1 Section will be at Starting Point with SAA Section closed up at 8.55 am.

4. ROUTE :- WATOU - POPERINGHE.

5. Billets :- All billets will be left clean and a certificate to this effect will be handed into this Headquarters at 8.45 am.

6. Baggage wagons will travel with their respective Sections.

7. Attention is called to D.A.O.O. No 111 dated 25.1.18.

8. Acknowledge.

                                Captain,
         Adjutant 50th Divisional Ammunition Column.
Issued at 5.0.pm 28.1.18.

Copy No 1 to War Diary.
Copy No 2 to No 1 Section.
Copy No 3 to No 2 Section.
Copy No 4 to SAA Section.
Copy No 5 to R.S.M.
Copies 6 & 7 Spare

SECRET.	Reference Map Sheet 28
	Edition 3., 1/40.000.

Copy No. 1....

OPERATION ORDER NO 36 by Lieut Colonel R.C. DRURY, R.F.A.
Commanding 50th Divisional Ammunition Column.
───

1. 50th D.A.C. will relieve 33rd D.A.C. as per table attached on 30.1.18.

2. Camps will be left clean and certificate to this effect will be handed into this office on arrival in new area.

3. A distance of 25 yards will be maintained between every 6 vehicles.

4. ACKNOWLEDGE.

Dean Captain.
Adjutant 50th D.A.C.

Issued at 7.pm 29.1.18.

Copy No 1 to War Diary
Copy No 2 to No 1 Section.
Copy No 3 to No 2 Section.
Copy No 4 to SAA Section.
Copy No 5 to R.S.M.
Copy No 6 Spare.

TABLE referred to :-

Unit	Unit to be relieved	Starting point at		Route.
Headquarters 50th DAC	H.Q. 33rd DAC H.15.a.	Billet	10 am	BUSSEBOOM – OUDERDOM.
1st Section. 50th DAC	1st Section 33rd DAC. H.15.a.	do	10.15 am	do do
SAA Sec: 50th DAC	SAA Sec: 33rd DAC H.16.a.	do	10.30 am	Cross roads G.15.b.17.– POPERINGHE – VLAMERTINGHE road –VLAMERTINGHE.
2nd Sec: 50th DAC	2nd Sec: 33rd DAC G.10.a.	do	10.45 am	Cross Roads. G.15.b.7.

SECRET   Copy No... 1

OPERATION ORDER No 33 by Lieut Colonel R.C. DRURY., R.F.A.
Commanding 50th Divisional Ammunition Column.

1. The 50th D.A.C. will march to CAMPAGNE AREA on 27.1.18.

2. Order of March :-
    Headquarters
    No 1 Section.
    No 2 Section
    SAA Section.

3. Starting point :-
    Headquarter Billet MERCK ST LIEVIN   7 am.
    No 1 Section School   -do-   6.45 am
    No 2 do   Billet   -do-   7.0 am
    SAA Section   do   -do-   7.15 am

No 2 Section and SAA Section will be in readiness to move at 6.45 am

4. Route :- OUVE-WIRQUIN - NOIRECORNET - BLENDEQUES.

5. Billets :- All billets will be left clean and a certificate to this effect will be handed in to this Headquarter at 6.45 am.

6. Baggage Wagons will travel with their respective Sections

7. Attention is called to D.A.O.O. No 111 dated 25.1.18.

8. ACKNOWLEDGE.

                                    Dean Captain.
                    Adjutant 50th Divisional Ammunition Column.
Issued at 6.0.pm 26.1.18.

Copy No 1 to War Diary.
Copy No 2 to No 1 Section.
Copy No 3 to No 2 Section.
Copy No 4 to SAA Section.
Copy No 5 to R.S.M.
Copies 6 & 7 Spare.

Copy No 1.

Operation Orders No 32 by Lieut Col R.C.DRURY., R.F.A.
Commanding 50th Divisional Ammunition Column.
for 15th January. 1918.

1. The D.A.C. will march to THIEMBRONNE Area via ARQUES WIZERNES and CLETY.

2. Billeting parties will leave at 6.45 a.m.
They will meet Lieut CLARKE at the HALTE (S.30.b.46 Sheet 27).

3. Headquarters will move at 9.15 a.m.

No 1 Section will be ready to move at 9 a.m. and will follow Headquarters, but will halt on reaching SAA section

SAA and No 2 Sections will be hooked in at the same time 9 a.m. and will join the Column when it passes them.
The order of March will be S.A.A. - No 2 - No 1.
The Column will enter ARQUES by the AIRE-ARQUES Road.

4. A C K N O W L E D G E.

C H Jose
Lieut.
a/Adjutant 50th D.A.C.

Issued at 7.15 p.m 14.1.18.

Copy No 1. War Diary.
Copy No 2. 1st Section.
Copy No 3. 2nd Section.
Copy No 4. SAA Section.
Copy No 5. R.S.M.
Copy No 6. Spare.

SECRET.   Copy No 1.

Operation Order No 31 by Lieut Col R.C.Drury., R.F.A.
Commanding 50th Divisional Ammunition Column.
for 14.1.18.

1.   The D.A.C. will move to RENESCURE. The route will be via WEMAERS CAPEL and ZUYTREENE and not as originally given.

2.   No 1 Section will be halted ready to move at 9.15 a.m. in the road running through J.14.a. just North of the X Road J.14.a.63.
SAA Section will follow No 1 Section.
No 2 Section will be halted ready to move in the road just N.W. of the X Road J.14.a.41 at 9.10 a.m.
Headquarters will be in the road J.14.c. at 9.15 a.m.
No 2 Section will follow Headquarters.

3.   The billeting parties will leave for RENESCURE as early as possible.

4.   Billeting Distribution Lists stating accommodation for Officers and Men must be sent to this office tonight without fail.

5.   A.S.C. Baggage Wagons must be returned to Refilling Point by the Church OUDERZEELE by 5.30 a.m. tomorrow 14th instant.

6.   A C K N O W L E D G E.

                                                 Lieut
                                   a/Adjutant 50th D. A. C.

Ref   Sheet 27.

Issued at 6.30 p.m. 13.1.18.

Copy No 1.   War Diary.
"   "   2.   1st Section.
"   "   3.   2nd   "
"   "   4.   SAA   "
"   "   5.   R.S.M.
"   "   6.   Spare.

Secret.   Copy No 1

OPERATION ORDER No 30 by Lieut Colonel R.C. DRURY, R.F.A.
Commanding 50th Divisional Ammunition Column.
─────────────────────

1. On the 13th instant the 50th D. A. C. will march to STEENVOORDE area.

2. Headquarters will be ready to move into the road from POPERINGHE as soon as the last vehicle of A & B/250 Bde have moved from lines.

3. No 2 Section will follow Headquarters when they move out. They will halt at the X Roads G.15.b.16. to allow the 1st Section to come in between No 2 Section and Headquarters.

4. No 1 Section will pull out when Headquarters is past their lines.

5. SAA Section will follow No 2 Section.

6. Sections will be harnessed ready to move at 8.30 am.

7. The lorries will leave under Lieut WHYTE.

8. Leading parties of 2 men with three days rations will be provided.

9. The lorries will proceed straight to THIEMBRONNE.

10. Rear parties, consisting of 1 N.C.O. and 2 men per Section, will be left behind to clear up camp.

11. Attention is called to attached.

12. ACKNOWLEDGE.

                                                        Lieut
                                a/Adjutant 50th Divisional Ammunition Column.
Issued at 5.30 pm 12.1.18.

Copy No 1 to War Diary.
 "   " 2 " No 1 Section.
 "   " 3 " No 2 Section.
 "   " 4 " SAA Section.
 "   " 5 " R.S.M.
 "   " 6 " Spare.

SECRET   Copy No 1.

OPERATION ORDER NO 29 by Lieut Colonel R.C. DRURY, R.F.A.
Commanding 50th Divisional Ammunition Column.

For 8th inst.

34 G.S. Wagons and teams are required from the D.A.C., 17 for Headquarters and Batteries of 250 Bde R.F.A., 17 for Headquarters and Batteries 251 Bde R.F.A.

No 1 Section will provide 7 wagons (To include the wagons already supplied to Batteries) and 12 teams and will draw 10 G.S. xxxxx Wagons and 5 teams from SAA Section.

No 2 Section will provide 7 wagons (to include the wagons already supplied to Batteries) and 7 teams and will draw 10 Wagons and 10 teams from SAA Section.

The teams and wagons will be distributed as follows :-

No 1 Section			No 2 Section	
1	to 250 Bde H.Q.		1	to 251 Bde H.Q.
4	to A/250		4	to A/251
4	to B/250		4	to B/251
4	to C/250		4	to C/251.
4	to D/250.		4	to D/251.

The wagons will report as above not later than 3 pm on 8th inst: The wagons will be left with the Batteries, the teams will return.

SAA Section will have teams and wagons ready for No 1 Section at 2 pm., and No 2 Section at 12 noon.

O.C. No 2 Section will also send up by his G.S. wagons, harness and drivers to complete the 30 mules already furnished by him to SAA Section as 6 mule teams.

3 N.C.Os will be supplied by No 1 Section.
3 N.C.Os do do do do 2 Section.
2 N.C.Os do do do do SAA Section.
To take charge of the various parties.

The wagons supplied for Divisional Arty Headquarters will return in time to be available for the batteries.

Map locations for the various batteries (1/40,000 Sheet 28) are enclosed.

FOR 9th inst.-

The teams for Batteries of 250 and 251 Bdes R.F.A. will report to them as under.
No 1 Section, 250 Bde R.F.A at 6.15 am.
No 2 Section 251 Bde R.F.A at 6.45 am

The 50th D.A.C. will relieve 33rd D.A.C. at the lines now occupied by the 33rd D.A.C.

No 1 Section and SAA Section will move at 8.30 am and 8.15 am respectively.

No 2 Section will arrange with O.C. No 2 Section 33rd D.A.C. to exchange wagon Lines after the completion of the Divl Arty move.

O.C. Sections will detail an Officer and an advance party of 3 O.Rs to proceed to new wagon lines on the 8th and take over wagon lines from the relieving unit.

Sections will at once report completion of their relief.

ACKNOWLEDGE.

CV Jone Lieut.
a/Adjutant 50th Divisional Ammunition Column.

Issued at 9.0.pm 7.1.18.

Copy No 1 to War Diary.
Copy No 2 to No 1 Section.
Copy No 3 to No 2 Section.
Copy No 4 to SAA Section.
Copy No 5 to R.S.M.
Copy No 6   Spare.

Map Locations referred to.
_____

H.Q. 250 Bde R.F.A.   ASYLUM YPRES.
A/250 Bde R.F.A.   H.16.d.58.
B/250   do   H.17.c.55
C/250   do   H.16.a.82
D/250   do   ASYLUM, YPRES.

@@@@@@@@@@@@@@@@@@@@@@@

H.Q. 251 Bde R.F.A.   H.9.d.68.
A/251   do   H.9.d.95.
B/251   do   H.11.d.86.
C/251   do   H.10.c.32.
D/250   do   H.9.d.86.

@@@@@@@@@@@@@@@@@@@@@@@@@@

CONFIDENTIAL:—

WAR DIARY

OF

50th DIVISIONAL AMMUNITION COLUMN

FROM 1-2-18 TO 28-2-18

VOLUME No XXXV

Army Form C. 2118.

WAR DIARY

50th DIVISIONAL AMMUNITION COLUMN

INTELLIGENCE SUMMARY

(Erase heading not required.)

VOLUME XXXV

Instructions regarding War Diaries and Intelligence Summaries are contained in F. S. Regs., Part II and the Staff Manual respectively. Title pages will be prepared in manuscript.

Place	Date	Hour	Summary of Events and Information	Remarks and references to Appendices
VLAMERTINGHE	1918 Feby 1st to 21st		Nothing to report beyond ordinary routine work.	
	22nd		The unit was relieved by 33rd D.A.C. The unit marched to OUDEZEELE.	O.Order No 37 attached
	24th		The unit marched to RENESCURE.	Order No 38 attached
	25th		The unit marched to THIEMBRONNE (rest over) HQ and 3rd Section billeted in (MERCK-ST-LIEVIN.) 1st Section " CLOQUANT and LA BUCAILLE 2nd Section " WIRQUIN	O. Order No 39 attached
	26th to 21st		Resting and Preparing for moving. Returns to O.C. R.F.A. Corps 50th Division	

SECRET
~~SECRET~~

Ref: Map HAZEBROUCK 5a.
Copy No. 1

OPERATION ORDER NO 38 By Lieut Colonel R.C.DRURY., R.F.A.
Commanding 50th Divisional Ammunition Column.

1. The 50th D.A.C. will march to RENESCURE on 24.2.18.

2. Order of March:-
   Headquarters.
   No.2 Section.
   No.1 Section.
   SAA Section.

3. Starting Point.
   Headquarters--Head of Column at Church, OUDEZEELE at 7-50a.m. followed by No.2 Section.
   No.1Section--Head of Section at Cross Roads, 1000 Yards North of O in OUDEZEELE at 8-10a.m.
   S.A.A.Section will close up to normal distance behind No. 1Section.

4. ROUTE:- LE-TEMPLE - OXELAERE - BAVINCHOVE.

5. BILLETS:- All billets will be left clean and a certificate to this effect will be handed into this Office on arrival at RENESCURE.

6. Baggage Wagons will travel with their respective Sections.

7. Attention of Section Commanders is drawn to 50th.D.A.O.O. No.114.

8. ACKNOWLEDGE.

Issued at 3-30 p.m. 23-2-18.

Captain,
Adjutant 50th.D.A.C.

Copy No.1 to War Diary.
Copy No.2 to No.1 Section.
Copy No.3 to No.2 Section.
Copy No.4 to S.A.A. Section.
Copy No.5 to R.S.M.
Copy No.6 Spare.

SECRET　　　　　　　　　　　　　　　　　　　　Ref: Map HAZEBROUCK 5a.
　　　　　　　　　　　　　　　　　　　　　　　Copy No 1

OPERATION ORDER NO 37 By Lieut Colonel R.C.DRURY., R.F.A.
Commanding 50th Divisional Ammunition Column.

1. The 50th D.A.C. will be relieved by the 33rd D.A. on 22.2.18, and will march to OUDEZEELE same date.

2. Order of March :-
   Headquarters.
   No 1 Section.
   SAA Section.
   No 2 Section.

3. Starting Point.
   Headquarters and No 1 Section - present Camp.
   Headquarters will leave Camp at 9.45 am followed by No 1 Section.
   Head of SAA Section to be at VLAMERTINGHE STATION at 10.25 am.
   No 2 Section :- Head of Section at Cross Roads. 300 yards North of E in POPERINGHE at 11.45 am

4. ROUTE :- VLAMERTINGHE - POPERINGHE - WATOU.

5. BILLETS :- All billets will be left clean and a certificate to this effect will be handed into this Office on arrival at OUDEZEELE.

6. Baggage Wagons will travel with their respective Sections.

7. A distance of 25 yards between every 6 vehicles will be maintained until the rear of the Column is past WATOU, then vehicles will close up to normal distances.

8. Attention is called to 50th D.A.O.O. No 114.

9. ACKNOWLEDGE.

Issued at 11 am 20.2.18.
　　　　　　　　　　　　　　　　　　　　　　　Captain,
　　　　　　　　　　　　　　　　　　　Adjutant 50th D.A.C.

Copy No 1 to War Diary.
Copy No 2 to No 1 Section.
Copy No 3 to No 2 Section.
Copy No 4 to SAA Section.
Copy No 5 to R.S.M.
Copy No 6 Spare.

Reference Map HAZEBROUCK 5 a.

SECRET Copy No. 1

OPERATION ORDER No 39 by Lieut Colonel, R.C.D URY., R.F.A.
Commanding 50th Divisional Ammunition Column.

1. The 50th D.A.C. will march to ELNES Area on 25th February 1918.

2. Order of March.
   Headquarters
   SAA Section.
   No 2 Section.
   No 1 Section.

3. Starting Point.
   Road Junction 1500 yds north west of M in CAMPAGNE
   Headquarters, Head of Headquarters to be at Starting Point at 9.55am.
   SAA Section, Head of Section to be at Starting Point 10.0 am
   No 2 Section   "   "   "   "   "   "   10.10 am
   No 1 Section   "   "   "   "   "   "   10.20 am

4. ROUTE.
   ARQUES - BLENDECQUES - WIZERNES - LUMBRES.

5. BILLETS.
   All billets will be left clean and a certificate to this effect will be handed into this Office on arrival at LUMBRES.

6. Baggage Wagons will travel with their respective Sections.

7. Attention of Section Commanders is drawn to 50th D.A.O.O. No 114.

8. ACKNOWLEDGE.

24 2 18

Captain
Adjutant, 50th D.A.C.

Copy No 1 to WAR DIARY.
Copy No 2 to No 1 Section.
Copy No 3 to No 2 Section.
Copy No 4 to SAA Section.
Copy No 5 to R.S.M.
Copy No 6 Spare.

50th (Northumbrian) Divisional Artillery.

50th DIVISIONAL AMMUNITION COLUMN R.F.A.

MARCH 1918

Army Form C. 2118.

WAR DIARY
INTELLIGENCE SUMMARY.

50TH DIVISIONAL AMMUNITION COLUMN
VOLUME XXXVI
MARCH 1918

Vol 32

Place	Date	Hour	Summary of Events and Information	Remarks and references to Appendices
MERCK-ST. LIEVIN.	1918. Mar 1. to Mar 8.		Nothing to report except general routine work.	
	Mar 9		Headquarters and S.A.A. Section entrained at ST.OMER. 1st Section at ARQUES and No 2 Section at WIZERNES, and detrained following morning at MOREUIL & LONGEAU and BOVE's respectively, and marched to BERTAUCOURT.	OO 4040 attached
BERTAUCOURT	Mar 10		Unit marched to MARLY CAMP, LANEUVILLE; Headquarters billetted at CAPPY.	OO42 attached
CAPPY.	Mar 12		Unit marched to BRUSLE.	OO43 attached
BRUSLE	Mar 15. to Mar 21.		Section employed in doing fatigue work for 281 and 288 A.T. Coys.	
		11.0pm	Unit marched to BUIRE.	
			'A' Echelon commenced supplying ammunition to batteries.	
BUIRE.	22nd	11.30am.	Headquarters and 'A' Echelon marched to VILLERS CARBONNEL; SAA Section went to BARLEUX	
VILLERS-CARBONNEL	23rd	noon	Headquarters and 'A' Echelon marched to O.6. central, sheet 62c (DIÉNCOURT). SAA Section billetted at ASSEVILLERS and then marched to PROYART.	
DIENCOURT	24th	10 am	Headquarters and 'A' Echelon marched to CAPPY.	

WAR DIARY
50TH DIVISIONAL AMMUNITION COLUMN
INTELLIGENCE SUMMARY
(Erase heading not required.)

Army Form C. 2118.

Instructions regarding War Diaries and Intelligence Summaries are contained in F.S. Regs., Part II. and the Staff Manual respectively. Title pages will be prepared in manuscript.

Places	Date	Hour	Summary of Events and Information	Remarks and references to Appendices
CAPPY	1918 Mar. 25	1.5 a.m.	Headquarters and 'A' Echelon marched to PROYART.	
PROYART	26	11 a.m.	Headquarters marched to MARCELCAVE; 1st Section to BAYONVILLERS and SAA Section to BAYONVILLERS.	
MARCELCAVE	26		1st Section moved to WIENCOURT; 2nd Section to GUILLACOURT; SAA Section to CAIX.	
	27	2 p.m.	Headquarters marched to ST. NICHOLAS. 1st Section at HANGARD; 2nd Section at DOMART. SAA Section at CACHY.	
	28	7 p.m.	HQ marched to SOURDON; 'A' Echelon at SOURDON; SAA Section at BOVES.	
	29	11.30 a.m.	HQ marched to BOVES; 1st Section MONIDEE; 2nd Section CASTEL.	
	30	11 a.m.	HQ marched to SAINS-EN-AMIENOIS; 1st Section at BOVES; 2nd Section SAINS EN AMIENOIS. 1st Section moved to ST. FUSCHIEN; 2nd Section moved to DOMARTIN and SAA Section to HEBECOURT.	
	31		HQ at SAINS EN AMIENOIS. 1st Section ST FUSCHIEN; 2nd Section DOMARTIN. SAA Section marched out to Rest with the Infantry. Since 21st 'A' Echelon has been very busy supplying ammunition, both night and day, to the batteries. SAA Section on that date came under the orders of 'Q'.	

R.C. Drury
Lieut Col RFA
Commanding 50th D.A.C.

SECRET   Copy No. 1......

OPERATION ORDER No 40 BY CAPTAIN H.L. MEAGHER. R.F.A.
Commanding 50th Divisional Ammunition Column.
----

1. The 50th DAC will entrain and detrain in accordance with 50th D.A. O.O. No 115 Table 'A'

2. ROUTE TO ENTRAINING STATIONS.--
    Headquarters. OUVE WIRQUIN - CLETY - WIZERNES - St OMER.
    & SAA Section.

    Remainder of No 1 Section- OUVE WIRQUIN - CLETY - NOIR
                               CORNET - BLENDECQUES - ARQUES.

    Remainder of No 2 Section -REMILLY WIRQUIN - Cross Roads
                               700 yds West of B in BIENTQUES
                               - WIZERNES.

3. Os.C. Nos 1 and 2 Sections will arrange direct with Batteries of 250 and 251 Bdes RFA respectively as to when and where the vehicles detached will meet the batteries with which they are to travel.

4. Baggage wagons will travel with Headquarters of Sections.

5. Rations for consumption up to and including the 11th inst will be carried.

6. BILLETS --
    All billets will be left in a clean condition.

7. ACKNOWLEDGE.

Issued at 12.20 am 8.3.18.

for Captain.
Adjutant 50th DAC.

Copy No 1 to War Diary
Copy No 2 to No 1 Section.
Copy No 3 to No 2 Section.
Copy No 4 to SAA Section.
Copy No 5 to R.S.M.
Copy No 6 Spare.

SECRET   Copy No. 1.

OPERATION NO N 42 by Captain H.L.MEAGHER. R.F.A.
Commanding 50th Divisional Ammunition Column.
----

1. The 50th DAC will move to MARLY CAMP, LANEUVILLE on the 12th inst.

2. The head of the Column will leave BERTEAUCOURT by the road BERTEAUCOURT - DOMART at 9 am. The Order of march will be :-
    Headquarters.
    No 1 Section.
    No 2 Section.
    SAA Section.

3. Two motor busses will report at BERTEAUCOURT at 4pm today one will be available for No 2 Section and SAA Section and one for Headquarters and No 1 Section.

4. Enclosed is D.A. Operation Order giving route to be followed.

5. ACKNOWLEDGE.

                                      signature Lieut
                             a/Adjt 50th Divl Ammn Column.

Issued at 12 noon 11.3.18.

Copy No 1 to War Diary.
Copy No 2 to No 1 Section.
Copy No 3 to No 2 Section.
Copy No 4 to SAA Section.
Copy No 5 to R.S.M.
Copy No 6 Spare.

SECRET.   Copy. 1

Operation Order No 43 by Captain H.L.Meagher R.F.A.(T).
Commanding 50th Divisional Ammunition Column.
----

1. D.A.C. will march to BRUSLE Area by route laid down in
   D.A. Operation Order No 119.

2. The Order of March will be :-
         Headquarters.
         2nd Section.
         SAA Section.
         1st Section.

3. The Column will move off under Capt Common and will
   meet Headquarters at Cross Roads outside BRAY at
   12 (noon).

4. Operation Order No 119 enclosed.

5. Acknowledge.

                        H.L.Meagher Capt Lieut.
                        a/Adjutant 50th D.A.C.

Issued at 9.30 a.m. 15.5.18.

Copy No 1   War Diary.   Copy No 4. SAA Section.
 "   " 2   1st Section.   "   " 5. R.S.M.
 "   " 3   2nd Section.   "   " 6. Spare.

50th Divisional Artillery.

50th DIVISIONAL AMMUNITION COLUMN R.F.A.

APRIL 1918.

CONFIDENTIAL.

WAR DIARY

OF

50ᵀᴴ DIVISIONAL AMMUNITION COLUMN.

FROM — TO
1-4-18. — 30.4.18.

VOLUME XXXVII

Army Form C. 2118.

WAR DIARY 50th DIVISIONAL AMMUNITION COLUMN.
INTELLIGENCE SUMMARY.
(Erase heading not required.) Page 7 VOLUME XXVII APRIL 1918

Instructions regarding War Diaries and Intelligence Summaries are contained in F. S. Regs., Part II. and the Staff Manual respectively. Title pages will be prepared in manuscript.

Place	Date	Hour	Summary of Events and Information	Remarks and references to Appendices
SAINS EN AMIENOIS	1918 April 1 to April 3		Headquarters at SAINS EN AMIENOIS 2nd Section at DOMARTIN 1st Section 5T FUSCHIEN. Sections employed in carrying ammunition to batteries.	
	April 4		2nd Section moved to COTTENCHY	
	" 5		1st Section " " BOVES.	
	" 6		2nd Section " " BOVES.	
	Apl 4.7 8.		Sections busily employed in supplying ammunition to batteries.	
			The 2 Section relieved and march with 251 Brigade to CLAIRY	
	9th		Headquarters marched to PONT DE METZ	
			1st Section relieved and march with 250 Brigade to PONT DE METZ.	
	10th		Unit marched to DOMQUEUR.	
	11th		" " BLANGERMONT Area and are billeted as under:–	
			HQrs at BLANGERVAL. 1st Section BLANGERVAL 2nd Section BLANGERMONT.	
	12th		Unit march to SAINS LES PERNES	
	13th		" " " ST. HILAIRE.	
	14th		" " " LAPUGNOY	

SHEET. 2.

WAR DIARY 50th DIVISIONAL AMMUNITION COLUMN. Army Form C. 2118.

INTELLIGENCE SUMMARY.
(Erase heading not required.) Page II

Place	Date	Hour	Summary of Events and Information	Remarks and references to Appendices
LAPUGNOY	1918			
	Apl 15.		1st Section come under tactical command of 3RD DA.	
			2nd Section march to BOUDOU and are administered by 4th DA.	
	Apl 17		" " " to BAS RIEUX	
	" 21		" " move to GOSNAY. and come under orders of 55. DAC.	
	" 25		" " " to LE TAILLY and come under orders of 4th DA.	
	Apl 14 to 28.		1st & 2nd Sections employed in delivering ammunition to batteries.	
	29.		Unit marched out to NÉDON.	Operation Order No. 44 herewith.
	30th.		Unit marched to Entrainment Stations, as under	
			Headquarters & 1st Section . . . . PERNES	Operation Order No. 45 herewith.
			2nd Section . . . . LAPUGNOY.	
			Sections entrained with their own Brigades.	

Repzun
Lieut Colonel R.F.A.
Commanding 50th Divisional Ammunition Column

Secret copy. No 1.

Ref: Map Sheet 36B Edit 6

OPERATION ORDER No 4 by Lieut Colonel R.C.DRURY.R.F.A.
Commanding 50TH DIVISIONAL AMMUNITION COLUMN.
----

1. On relief of 50th D.A.C. by 14th D.A.C. on 28/29 and 29/30th April 1918 the 50th DAC will march to Billets at NEDON. B.8.a and c.
Headquarters, 1st and 2nd Sections will march independantly as soon as relief is complete

2. Billetting parties as under will proceed to Billeting Area on xxxxxxx morning of 28th inst and report to S.C.R.A. at 2 pm same day at D.A.H.Q. at AMETTES.
     1 Officer & 2 N.C.Os. per Section.

3. Sections will move with 18pdr and 4.5 How limbered Ammn wagons full.

4. Billets will be handed over and certificate of cleanliness obtained.

5. Attention is called to D.A.O.O. No 117 attached

6 ACKNOWLEDGE.

                                      Captain.
                        Adjutant 50th Divisional Ammunition
                                      Column.

Issued at 6pm 27.4.18.

Copy No 1 to War Diary
Copy No 2 to No 1 Section
Copy No 3 to No 2 Section
Copy No 4 to R.S.M.
Copy No 5 Spare.

SECRET.   COPY No. 1

OPERATION ORDER No 45 BY LT. COL.
R.C. DRURY, COMMANDING 50 D.A.C.
— for TUESDAY, 30.4.18 —

1. 50. D.A.C. will entrain at PERNES and LAPUGNOY, in accordance with DIVL ARTY Operation Order no 128.

2. Section Commanders will arrange direct with Brigade and Battery Commanders of their respective Brigades as to the time and place that the detached vehicles will meet the Battery to which they are allotted.

3. O.C. 1st Section will detail an Officer to proceed on Train No 1. and O.C. No 2 Section an Officer to proceed on Train No 2. These Officers will superintend the detraining of their Sections on Detraining Stations.

4. Units will be at entraining station 3 hours before departure of train.

5. Entraining States will be handed to the Officer superintending entraining, at the entraining point.

6. Attention is called to D.A.O.O. no 128 and entraining and detraining instructions issued herewith.

7. ACKNOWLEDGE.

Captain
Adjutant 50 D.A.C.
Issued at   29.4.18.

Copy no 1.   War Diary
"   " 2   1st Section
"   " 3   2nd.
"   " 4   RSM.
"   " 5   Spare.

CONFIDENTIAL

WAR DIARY

OF

50TH DIVISIONAL AMMUNITION COLUMN

FROM 1.5.18. TO 31.5.18.

VOLUME XXXVIII

Army Form C. 2118.

WAR DIARY 50TH DIVISIONAL AMMUNITION COLUMN.

INTELLIGENCE SUMMARY. MAY 1918. VOLUME XXXVIII

(Erase heading not required.)

Instructions regarding War Diaries and Intelligence Summaries are contained in F. S. Regs., Part II. and the Staff Manual respectively. Title pages will be prepared in manuscript.

Place	Date 1918	Hour	Summary of Events and Information	Remarks and references to Appendices
FERE EN TARDENOIS.	MAY 1.	6.0 pm.	Headquarters detrained and marched to COHAN at FERE EN TARDENOIS. 1st Section detrained at FISMES & marched to COHAN. 2nd Section detrained at SAVIGNY & marched to COHAN. SAA Section detrained at FERE & marched to IGNY L'ABBAYE.	O.O.46. attached
	4.	3.30 am.	Headquarters & batteries moved to BASLIEUX-LES-FISMES via BRAVIGNY- ST GILLES- FISMES and took over camp on BASLIEUX- COURLANDON Road.	
	5.		Sections supplying ammunition to Battery positions	
	10.			
	11.	1.30 pm.	Headquarters & Sections moved to GLENNES. SAA Section moved to MUSCOURT.	00/47 atta
	8.			
	11.			
	21.		Nothing to report beyond carrying out of daily fatigues.	
	27.	1.0 am.	Enemy commenced a heavy bombardment and sent over burying gas.	
		9.30 am.	Headquarters & Sections commenced to march out of GLENNES and were subjected to heavy hostile fire. Drivers ... shelled. It Other Ranks and 12 Other Ranks wounded.	

1577 Wt.W10791/1773 500,000 7/15 D.D.& L. A.D.S.S./Forms/C.2118.

WAR DIARY 50TH DIVISIONAL AMMUNITION COLUMN

INTELLIGENCE SUMMARY

Army Form C. 2118.

Page 2

Place	Date 1918	Hour	Summary of Events and Information	Remarks and references to Appendices
GLENNES	MAY 27		Missing 3 Officers. 17 Other Ranks who are believed Prisoners of war.	
		10pm	Arrived at ST GILLES.	
		60/m	Marched to DRAVEGNY. Column stood to all night.	
DRAVEGNY	28	9.30am	Marched to Bois de MEUNIERE, via COHAN- COLONGES- GOUSSANCOURT and bivouac in the wood. Beaulies:- Killed 1 man by E.A. bomb and 1 man wounded	
	29	3.0am	Marched to near BASLIEUX-SOUS-CHATILLON	
		6.40pm	Marched to IGNY LE-JARD arriving there about 2.0am 30th. via VANDIERES- VERNEUIL.	
	30	1.30pm	Marched to VERDON via LE BREUIL and bivouac in wood.	
	31	8.0am	Left VERDON at 8.45am and marched to COURJEONNET via MARGNY- JANVILLIERS- FROMENTIERES- CHAMPAUBERT- CONGY arriving at COURJEONNET at 4pm.	

Rebuey
Lieut Colonel R.F.A
Commanding 50th D.A.C

SECRET   Reference Map SOISSON 1/100.000

OPERATION ORDER No 47 by LIEUT COLONEL R.C. DRURY .R.F.A.
COMMANDING 50TH DIVISIONAL AMMUNITION COLUMN.
----

1. The 50th D. A. C. will move to GLENNES on 11.5.18.

2. Headquarters and Sections will move independently.

3. STARTING POINT.
Headquarters	Present Lines	1.30pm
No 1 Section	do	1.40pm
No 2 Section	do	2.30pm

4. Each Section will leave behind a rearparty of 1 Officer and 6 Other Ranks to clean up camp. When Camps are clean they will be handed over to Town Major and Certificate obtained. This certificate will be handed into this Office on arrival at GLENNES.

5. Notice Boards will be put into all stables showing that they have been disinfected.

6. ACKNOWLEDGE.

Issued at 6.pm 10.5.18.   Adjutant 50th D. A. C.
                                                    Captain.

Copy No 1 to War Diary
Copy No 2 to No 1 Section
Copy No 3 to No 2 Section
Copy No 4 to XX R.S.M.
Copy No 5 Spare

SECRET   Reference Map 1/100.000 SOISSONS.

OPERATION ORDER No 46 by LIEUT COLONEL R.C.DRURY.R.F.A.
COMMANDING 50TH DIVISIONAL AMMUNITION COLUMN.
----

1. The 50th D.A.C. will march tomorrow 5th instant to BASLIEUX I.3. North.Central.

2. Starting Point.
   Fork Roads 280 yards S.E. of N in COHAN

3. Order of March.
   Head of Column to be at Starting Point at
       Headquarters   3.30 am
       No 1 Section   3.35 am
       No 2 Section   3.55 am
       SAA Section   4.7 am

4. ROUTE :-
   St GILLES - FISMES

5. Sections will move at the normal distances as laid down in Field Service Regs, If the weather is fine and visibility good distance will be observed at the discretion of the C.O. of at least 500 metres between Sections in order to xxxixx avoid observation from the air.

6. Billets will be left clean and in a sanitary condition.

7. ACKNOWLEDGE .

                                              Captain.
                             Adjutant 50th D. A. C.

Issued at 10.0pm 4.5.18.

Copy No 1 to War Diary
Copy No 2 to No 1 Section.
Copy No 3 to No 2 Section.
Copy No 4 to X.X.X.SAA Section
Copy No 5 to R.S.M.
Copy No 6 Spare.

CONFIDENTIAL

WAR DIARY

OF

50TH DIVISIONAL AMMUNITION COLUMN.

FROM 1.6.18 TO 30.6.18.

VOLUME XXXIX

WAR DIARY 50TH DIVISIONAL AMMUNITION COLUMN. Army Form C. 2118.

INTELLIGENCE SUMMARY

JUNE 1918 /6C 35 VOLUME XXIX

Place	Date 1918	Hour	Summary of Events and Information	Remarks and references to Appendices
COURCONNET.	June 1.		6 Officers, 15 Gunners and 3 Signallers were sent to the Composite Artillery Brigade in formation. 2nd Section was brought up to establishment to act as Brigade Ammunition Column for Composite Artillery Brigade.	
	June 3	3/mild	Headquarters moved to JOCHES.	
	June 4		Orders were received for composite arts. section for Composite Infantry Brigade to be in readiness for move.	
	June 9		R.Q.B. marched to LES EPEES 3me, near LACHY via BROUSSY-LE-PETIT-MONDIMENT - CHAPTON- LACHY.	
	June 10		Composite Artillery Brigade was disbanded. All ranks returned with exception of officers.	
	June 17		3 Officers and 42 Other Ranks arrived from Base for Divisional Artillery.	
	June 21.		16 Officers received from Base. SAA Section	
	June 30	8.30am	D.A.C. marched to PLEURS	

WAR DIARY 50TH DIVISIONAL AMMUNITION COLUMN
or
INTELLIGENCE SUMMARY.
(Erase heading not required.)

Army Form C. 2118.

Place	Date	Hour	Summary of Events and Information	Remarks and references to Appendices
LES EPEES FME LACHY.			Whilst in the LES EPEES Fme. Area the re-equipping of the Unit was carried out: also training was done. On 23rd June a large number of men were taken ill with 'P.U.O.' A small hospital was established in the billets until the 27th. Usually there were from 50 to 60 patients in the hospital. After that date all cases were removed to Field Ambulance.	

RH Moy
Lieut Colonel R.F.A.
Commanding 50th Divisional Ammunition Column

WAR DIARY 50TH DIVISIONAL AMMUNITION COLUMN

INTELLIGENCE SUMMARY

JULY 1918. VOL XL

Army Form C. 2118.

Place	Date 1918	Hour	Summary of Events and Information	Remarks and references to Appendices
LACHY.	July 1st	9.0 a.m.	Headquarters marched to FLEURS via BROYES – PEAS.	
PLEURS.	2nd		S.A.A. Section marched to MAILLY LE CAMP via OGNES – GOURGANÇON.	
PLEURS.	2nd		Headquarters marched to MAILLY LE CAMP via OGNES – GOURGANÇON.	
LACHY			1st Section marched to CONNANTRE via BROYES – ST LOUP.	
LACHY			2nd Section marched to LENHARREE via BROYES – BANNES.	
MAILLY.	3rd	11 a.m.	½ S.A.A. Section entrained at MAILLY LE CAMP and detrained at LONGPRÉ on July 4th; and marched to ALLERY.	
		8 a.m.	½ S.A.A Section entrained at MAILLY LE CAMP and detrained at LONGPRÉ on July 4th; and marched to ALLERY.	
		5 p.m.	½ Headquarters entrained at MAILLY LE CAMP and detrained at PONT REMY on July 4th; and marched to ALLERY.	
FERE-CHAMPENOISE.			½ 1st Section entrained at FERE-CHAMPENOISE and detrained at HANGEST on July 4th; and marched to ALLERY.	
SOMMESOUS.			½ 2nd Section entrained at SOMMESOUS and detrained at LONGPRÉ on July 4th; and marched to ALLERY.	

SECRET

Copy No 1.

Ref: Map VIGNACOURT ADMINISTRATIVE
1/100,000.

OPERATION ORDER NO: 48 by LIEUT COLONEL R.C. DRURY.R.F.A.
COMMANDING 50TH DIVISIONAL AMMUNITION COLUMN.

1. The 50 D.A.C. will march to BELLOY AREA on 28th JULY 1918.

2. Order of March :-

	Starting Point	Hour.
Headquarters	Section Lines	8.30 am
No 1 Section	do	8.34 am
No 2 Section	do	8.49 am
SAA Section	do	9. 5 am.

3. ROUTE :- LONGPRE - FLIXECOURT.

4. BILLETING PARTIES of 1 Officer and 1 N.C.O. per Headquarters and Sections will meet the Staff Captain at Area Commandants Office BELLOY at 9 am on 28th inst.

5. MARCH DISCIPLINE --
Strict March Discipline will be maintained enforced, and the following distances will be maintained throughout the whole journey.
  Between Sections   100 yds
     do   every 6 vehicles   25 yds.

6. REAR PARTIES :-
A rear Party of 1 Officer from No 1 Section and 6 Other Ranks per Section will be left behind to clean up camp and receive a certificate of cleanliness from the Billet Warden for the whole of the Camp occupied by the Unit.
The Certificate will be handed into this Office on completion of journey.

7. Attention is drawn to D.A.O.O. No 133 attached.

8. ACKNOWLEDGE.

Issued at 7.25 pm 27.7.18.

Captain.
Adjutant.50th Divl Ammn Column.

Copy No 1 to War Diary.
Copy No 2 to No 1 Section.
Copy No 3 to No 2 Section.
Copy No 4 to SAA Section.
Copy No 5 to R.S.M.
Copy No 6 Spare.

WAR DIARY
50TH DIVISIONAL AMMUNITION COLUMN
INTELLIGENCE SUMMARY

Army Form C. 2118.

Place	Date 1918	Hour	Summary of Events and Information	Remarks and references to Appendices
MAILLY	July 4th	1 am.	Remainder of Headquarters entrained and detrained at PONT REMY on 5th July; and marched to ALLERY.	
FERE CHAMPENOISE			Remainder of 1st Section entrained and detrained at HANGEST on 5th July; and marched to ALLERY.	
SOMMESOUS			Remainder of 2nd Section entrained and detrained at LONGPRÉ on July 5th and marched to ALLERY.	
ALLERY	July 5. to July 27th.		nothing to report beyond ordinary routine work and training.	
	July 28.	8.30 am.	Headquarters and Sections marched to BELLOY-SUR-SOMME via BETTENCOURT - LONGPRÉ - FLIXICOURT.	Appendix 20/1 O.O 48 attached
BELLOY SUR SOMME	July 29th to 31st		nothing to report beyond ordinary routine work.	

R.C.Druey
Lieut Colonel R.F.A.
Commanding 50th Divisional Ammunition Column

PAGE 1.

Army Form C. 2118.

WAR DIARY of 50th Divisional Ammunition Co
50TH DIVISIONAL AMMUNITION COLUMN
INTELLIGENCE SUMMARY.
(Erase heading not required.)

AUGUST 1918.   VOL XII

Vol 37

Instructions regarding War Diaries and Intelligence Summaries are contained in F. S. Regs., Part II. and the Staff Manual respectively. Title pages will be prepared in manuscript.

Place	Date	Hour	Summary of Events and Information	Remarks and references to Appendices
BELLOY SUR SOMME	1.8.18.		A.R.P. at FRECHENCOURT taken over from 4th Australian D.A.	
	2.8.18.	11am	Headquarters and Sections marched to FRECHENCOURT via ST VAAST - POULAINVILLE - ST. GRATIEN. New A.R.P. formed at HEILLY (J17d.54 Sheet 62D)	
FRECHENCOURT	3.8.18		Headquarters, 1st Section and 2nd Section marched to:- HQ. H16.6.76. 1st Section H12.c.55 2nd Section H16.c.55. Sheet 62D	
	4.8.18 to 7.8.18.		'A' Echelon assisted by SAA section when to full capacity in delivering ammunition to Brigades.	
	8.8.18		1st Section moved to I.12.c.74 (Sheet 62D) 2nd " " " I.24.a. central (Sheet 62D) Dump reformed at FRECHENCOURT transferred to Dump at J.20.c. (10mm).	
	9.8.18.		Headquarters moved to BONNAY. (I.17.d.05.65 Sheet 62D) 2nd Section moved to I.23.a.79.	
BONNAY	10.8.18		SAA Section moved to BONNAY (I17.d.37 Sheet 62D)	

WAR DIARY of 50TH DIVISIONAL AMMUNITION COLUMN

INTELLIGENCE SUMMARY.

(Erase heading not required.)

Army Form C. 2118.
PAGE 2

Place	Date	Hour	Summary of Events and Information	Remarks and references to Appendices
BONNAY	10.8.18		1st Section marched to J26.c.2b. 2nd " " " J26.c.0b. Headquarters " " J26.d.15 (VAUX-SUR-SOMME)	
VAUX SUR SOMME	11.8.18		R.A.A. Section marched to J26.c. A.R.P. formed at VAUX Ammunition for this dump drawn from Dumps J20.c and HEILLY	
	13.8.18		Salvage dump opened at J35d Commenced collecting J21. 22. 23 & 24 of gun ammunition	
	14.8.18		Salvage dump at J35d closed. New Salvage dump opened at J22.a.36 (sheet 62d) Area to be collected between K. and 15 of grid line through J24 central and 6 and 15 of grid line through J26.00	
	9.8.18 to 3.2.8.18		Sections delivering Ammunition to Brigades R.A.A. section assisted in salvage operations During period of salvage operations our 35,000 Rds of S.A.A. Ammunition were salved	

PAGE 3

WAR DIARY 50th DIVISIONAL AMMUNITION COLUMN

Army Form C. 2118.

INTELLIGENCE SUMMARY.

(Erase heading not required.)

Instructions regarding War Diaries and Intelligence Summaries are contained in F. S. Regs., Part II. and the Staff Manual respectively. Title pages will be prepared in manuscript.

Place	Date	Hour	Summary of Events and Information	Remarks and references to Appendices
VAUX-SUR-SOMME	22/8/18		J.35.d. A.R.P. transferred to J.22.a.	
	24/8/18		New A.R.P. formed at K.13.d.22.	
	25/8/18		VAUX A.R.P. closed.	
			1st Section marched to J.36.d.	
			2nd " " SAILLY LAURETTE.	
	26/8/18		New A.R.P. formed at K.17. central	
			Headquarters move to CHIPILLY (K.33.c.77)	
		6 p.m.	All A.R.P's are handed over to 58th D.A.	
			Unit comes under orders of 3rd Australian D.A.	
			1st Section moved to K.24.c.99	
	27/8/18		2nd Section moved to L.31.b.79	

PAGE 4

WAR DIARY 50TH DIVISIONAL AMMUNITION COLUMN
Army Form C. 2118.

INTELLIGENCE SUMMARY
(Erase heading not required.)

Instructions regarding War Diaries and Intelligence Summaries are contained in F. S. Regs., Part II. and the Staff Manual respectively. Title pages will be prepared in manuscript.

Place	Date	Hour	Summary of Events and Information	Remarks and references to Appendices
CHIPILLY	28.8.18		Headquarters moved to BRAY.	
			2nd Section " " L.24.a.	
			S.A.A. " " L.16.a.	
	29.8.18		1st Section moved to L.29.b.	
	30.8.18		Headquarters moved to G.17. central (Sheet 62c)	
			1st Section " CURLU	
			2nd " " VAUX	
			S.A.A. " BELLOY-SUR-SOMME and become under orders of G.H.Q. Reserve.	
	31.8.18. 2pm		Underseened to march to [crossed out] out of 3rd Australian D.A. Area.	
			Unit moved to ALBERT Area.	
			Headquarters on ALBERT-BOUZENCOURT Road	
			1st Section " ALBERT-BAPAUME Road	
			2nd " " BOUZENCOURT.	
			During the whole month all Sections were very busy supplying ammunition to Brigades, and also giving areas of gun and Howitzer ammunition to Several Anti-tank and machine guns kept in Reserve. also as much	

Lieut Colonel RFA
Commanding 50th Divl Ammunition Column

Vol 38

WAR DIARY

OF

50TH DIVISIONAL

AMMUNITION COLUMN.

FOR

SEPTEMBER 1918

VOLUME XLI.

30TH SEPT 1918.

PAGE: 1

Army Form C. 2118.

WAR DIARY 50th DIVISIONAL AMMUNITION Column

INTELLIGENCE SUMMARY.

(Erase heading not required.)

Instructions regarding War Diaries and Intelligence Summaries are contained in F. S. Regs., Part II. and the Staff Manual respectively. Title pages will be prepared in manuscript.

Place	Date	Hour	Summary of Events and Information	Remarks and references to Appendices
ALBERT	1.9.18	11 am	Headquarters and 'A' Echelon moved to FAMECHON	
FAMECHON	2.9.18		Headquarters and 'A' Echelon moved to 'CITADELLE' ARRAS, via LA BELLE VUE.	
	3.9.18		All Section moved to HAUTE VISÉE from DELLOY-SUR-SOMME.	
	5.9.18		Headquarters move to H.28.c., Sheet 51B. & take over from 15th D.A.C. 1st Section " H.34.a " 2nd " H.33.b "	
ARRAS	10.9.18		Headquarters and 'A' Echelon relieved by 11th D.A.C and marched to Headquarters. G. 16.d.15., Sheet 51B 1st Section G. 19.b. 2nd Section G. 19.a	
	13.9.18		No 1. Section take over lines of 49th DAC at G.26.a. central	

PAGE 2

WAR DIARY 50th DIVISIONAL AMMUNITION COLUMN.
Army Form C. 2118.

INTELLIGENCE SUMMARY.

(Erase heading not required.)

Place	Date	Hour	Summary of Events and Information	Remarks and references to Appendices
ARRAS	14.9.18		Headquarters taken over from 49th D.A.C. at G.26.b.77 2nd Section moved to G.26.a. central. Salvage operations commenced, area being H. and S. of the Scarpe divided up as follows:- (a) NORTHERN. N. of SCARPE South of E. and W. Grid line from B.25.c.00 to C.26.c.00 (b) SOUTHERN. S. of SCARPE between rivers and ARRAS-CAMBRAI Road as far eastward as VIZ-EN-ARTOIS.	
	15.9.18 to 22.9.18		During this period several thousands of rounds of 9.2"Hows, 8"Hows, 6"Hows 60.Pdr, 4.5", 18 Pdrs and T.M. Ammunition were salved and sent to MAIN DUMPS; German ammunition was also salved; also several thousands of 18 Pdr and 4.5" 460Pdr cartridge cases, S.A.A. and ammunition boxes. In addition to the above the following were salved:- 5.. German 5'9" Hows 3.. Heavy T.Mortars 1.. Medium " 1.. Light "	
	22.9.18		Relieved from Salvage Operations	
	18.9.16		3rd Section moved to MILLY	

PAGE 3

WAR DIARY 50TH DIVISIONAL AMMUNITION COLUMN.

INTELLIGENCE SUMMARY.

(Erase heading not required.)

Place	Date	Hour	Summary of Events and Information	Remarks and references to Appendices
ARRAS.	22.9.18		2nd Section moved to U.19.a.5.3 and become attached to 4th Canadian D.A.	
	23.9.18		1st Section moved to H.33.b. central and become attached to 56th D.A	
	24.9.18		1st Section moved to CHERISY.	
	30.9.18		2nd Section moved to INCHY-	
	30.9.18		1st Section moved to GAGNICOURT	

[signature] Captain
Commanding 50th D.A.C.

War Diary

of

50th Divisional

Ammunition Column

For

October 1918

Volume XIII

31st October 1918

PAGE No 1. 50th DIVISIONAL AMMUNITION COLUMN
Army Form C. 2118.

WAR DIARY

INTELLIGENCE SUMMARY

Place	Date	Hour	Summary of Events and Information	Remarks and references to Appendices
	1.10.18		2nd Section moved to BOURLON WOOD S.A.A.", who are detached from Headquarters and 'A' Echelon, moved to MURLU after having stayed at COMBLES for 4 days.	
	2.10.18		1st and 2nd Section moved out of forward area to ARRAS-DOULLENS Road ARRAS.	
	3.10.18		S.A.A. Section moved to LIERAMONT.	
	5.10.18		S.A.A. Section moved to EPEHY.	
ARRAS.	6.10.18		LA TARGETTE and PANET DUMP (LA TARGETTE and ABLAIN ST NAZAIRE) taken over from 20th D.A.C.	
	7.10.18	11.50	Headquarters and 'A' Echelon relieved 20th D.A.C. at GOUY-SERVINS	0051 attached
GOUY SERVINS	8.10.18		Headquarters and 'A' Echelon moved to CARENCY	

PAGE. 2.

WAR DIARY 50TH DIVISIONAL AMMUNITION COLUMN
INTELLIGENCE SUMMARY

Army Form C. 2118.

(Erase heading not required.)

Instructions regarding War Diaries and Intelligence Summaries are contained in F.S. Regs., Part II. and the Staff Manual respectively. Title pages will be prepared in manuscript.

Place	Date	Hour	Summary of Events and Information	Remarks and references to Appendices
	9.10.18		S.A.A. Section moved to LE CATELET.	
	10.10.18		S.A.A Section moved to P.26.b.43 Sheet 57B.	
CARENCY			Gas dump formed at M31.c.98 Sheet 44A (COULOTTE)	
	12.10.18		Headquarters and 'A' Echelon moved to FREVIN CAPELLE after being relieved by 12th D.A.C. All dumps handed over	
FREVIN CAPELLE	14.10.18	12.47	H.Q. entrained at ACQ – Arrived TINCOURT at 00.01. 15.10.18.	00.52 attached
			1st Section " " AUBIGNY – Arrived PERONNE.	
			1st " " " ACQ – Arrived TINCOURT.	
			Headquarters and 'A' Echelon marched to TEMPLEUX-LE-FOSSE	
	16.10.18		2nd Section moved to DRIENCOURT	

PAGE No. 3

WAR DIARY 50TH DIVISIONAL AMMUNITION COLUMN

INTELLIGENCE SUMMARY

Place	Date	Hour	Summary of Events and Information	Remarks and references to Appendices
TEMPLEUX LE FOSSE	19.10.18		Headquarters and 'A' Echelon moved to BEAUREVOIR.	OO 53 attd/
BEAUREVOIR	20.10.18		Headquarters moved to MARETZ 1st Section moved to P27.c.57 Sheet 57ᴰ P2.a.96. " 2nd " "	
MARETZ	23.10.18		1st Section moved to K.28.c.75 Sheet 57ᴮ K.23.d.37 " 2nd " "	
MARETZ	25.10.18		Headquarters moved to K28.b.75 Sheet 57ᴮ	
MONTAY	28.10.18		1st Section moved to K24.a.76 Sheet 57ᴮ K.24.d.50 " 2nd " "	
	29.10.18		SAA Section moved to K.27.b.50 Sheet 57ᴮ	

PAGE 4

WAR DIARY 50TH DIVISIONAL AMMUNITION COLUMN

INTELLIGENCE SUMMARY

Army Form C. 2118.

Place	Date	Hour	Summary of Events and Information	Remarks and references to Appendices
MONTAY	31.10.18		1 Officer and 15 Other Ranks sent to Ammunition Dump at L.13.b. Sheet 57c. and come under orders of 18th D.A.	
			During the month Sections were kept exceedingly busy in supplying ammunition to Batteries, thus maintaining a good supply of ammunition. Many remounts have been collected from Remount Depots.	

R.C.Bury
Lieut Colonel RFA
Commanding 50th Divl Ammn Column

Secret.

Copy No 1.

Operation Order No 51 by Captain J. DEAN., RFA.,
Commanding 50th Divisional Ammunition Column.

Ref Map Sheet :
1:100,000 LENS 11.

1.   50th D.A.C. will relieve 20th D.A.C. on 7.10.18.

    20th D.A.C.
        Headquarters.   W.5.b.35   Sheet 44B.
        1st Section.   W.5.b.37.   "   "
        2nd Section.   W.5.d.29.   "   "

2. ORDER OF MARCH ---

	Starting Point.	Head of Column to pass Starting Point at :-
Headquarters.	Present Lines.	0915.
2nd Section.	" "	0917.
1st Section.	" "	0927.

3. ROUTE ---
    ANZIN-ST AUBIN- Cross Roads CHAUSSEE- VILLERS-AU-BOIS.

4. ADVANCE PARTIES ---
    Each Section will send BQMS or assistant to take over their respective camps from 20th D.A.C., and will report to 20th DAC at 1000.

5. REAR PARTIES ---
    As rear parties cannot be left behind to hand over to Billet Wardens, Sections will ensure that billets are clean, and will leave a representative to obtain the necessary certificate from the Area Commandant for their respective camps.

6.   Attention is called to D.A.Q.O. No 141 herewith.

7.   A c k n o w l e d g e.

                                                    2nd Lieut.
                                        Adjutant 50th D. A. C.

Issued at   1150   6.10.18.

Copy No 1.   War Diary.
  "   " 2.   1st Section.
  "   " 3.   2nd Section.
  "   " 4 & 5. Spare.

SECRET.   Copy No 1.

Operation Order No 52 by Lieut Col R.C.Drury., RFA.
Commanding 50th Divisional Ammunition Column.
for Monday, & Tuesday 14/15th October, 1918.
_____

1. 50th D. A. C. will entrain at ACQ and AUBIGNY in accordance with Entrainment Statement issued with 50th D.A. Administrative Instructions dated 12.10.18.

2. Section Commanders will arrange direct with Brigade and Battery Commanders of their respective Brigades as to the time and place that the detached vehicles will meet the Battery to which they are allotted *for entrainment*.

3. Os.C. Sections will detail the undermentioned officers to superintend entraining of their respective sections :-
   1st Section.   2nd Lieut E.J.Berryman., MC.
   2nd Section.   Lieut J.W.Hillyard.

   These Officers will report to R.T.O. two hours before the first unit arrives at each entraining station and will remain in touch with the R.T.O. throughout entrainment. Entraining Officers will leave with the last train from their respective stations.

4. Os.C. Sections will detail the undermentioned officers to superintend detraining :-
   1st Section.   2nd Lieut Leeming.
   2nd Section.   2nd Lieut Wright.

   These officers will proceed by the first train which leaves First Army Area.

5. Os.C. Sections will each detail the following billeting party, who will travel by first train leaving First Army Area :-
   Headquarters.   M. Lerch.   1 N.C.O.
   1st Section.   2/Lt W.Baird.   1 N.C.O.
   2nd Section.   Lieut Clarke.   1 N.C.O.

6. 2nd Lieut Ravenscroft will be attached to No 1 Section, until the move has been completed, when he will return to No 2 Section.

7. Attention is drawn to 50th D.A. Administrative Instructions of 12.10.18 and entraining and detraining instructions issued herewith.

8. A c k n o w l e d g e .

                                               2nd Lieut.
                                  Adjutant 50th Divl Ammunition Column.

Issued at 16.00 hours 13.10.18.

   Copy No 1   War Diary.
    "   " 2   1st Section.
    "   " 3   2nd Section.
    "   " 4   Spare.
    "   " 5   Spare.

SECRET.   Copy No ..../

Operation Order No 53 by Lieut Colonel R.C.Drury., RFA.
Commanding 50th Divisional Ammunition Column.
for Saturday 19th October, 1918.

Ref Map Sheets 62C and 62B, 1:40,000 .

1.   50th D.A.C. will march to BEAUREVOIR Area tomorrow 19.10.18.

2.   ORDER OF MARCH ---

	Starting Point.	Head of Column to pass Starting Point at :-
Headquarters.	Cross Roads at J.4.d.55, Sheet 62C.	0930 .
1st Section.	Ditto.	0933 .
2nd Section.	Ditto.	0943 .

3.   ROUTE ---
ROISEL - HARGICOURT - BELLICOURT .

4.   BILLETING PARTIES ---
Billeting Parties detailed as under will meet Staff Captain at Area Commandant's Office, BEAUREVOIR at 1100 hours .
After receiving instructions they will meet their respective Sections and Headquarters at BELLICOURT and guide them to their destination .

        1st Section.   1 Officer & 1 N.C.O.
        2nd Section.   1 Officer & 1 N.C.O.

O.C. 1st Section will detail Lieut SKENE x to act as Billeting Officer for Headquarters .

5.   REAR PARTIES ---
Rear parties detailed as under will remain behind to clean up the billets and lines. The Officer i/c will obtain a certificate from the Area Commandant to the effect that the camps have been handed over in a clean and sanitary condition. Certificate to be forwarded to this office .

        2nd Section.   1 Officer.   1 N.C.O. 3 O.Rks.
        1st Section .   1 N.C.O. 3 O.Rks.

Area Commandant at NURLU has been advised of time of depart-ure and requested to have representatives at the Camps by 0900 .

6.   MARCH DISCIPLINE ---
Special attention will be paid to march discipline and the following distances will be maintained :-
        Between Sections.   100 yards .
        Between every six vehicles.   25 yards .
Attention is drawn to 4th Army R.O. No 2039 .

7.   A C K N O W L E D G E .

                                                                  2nd Lieut.
                            Adjutant 50th Divisional Ammunition Column.

Issued at 2225   18.10.18.
    Copy No 1.   War Diary .
    Copy No 2.   1st Section.
    Copy No 3 .   2nd Section.
    Copies 4 & 5.   Spare .

WAR DIARY

OF

50TH DIVISIONAL

AMMUNITION COLUMN.

FOR.

NOVEMBER, 1918.

VOLUME. XLIII.

30th November, 1918.

PAGE No 1

WAR DIARY 50th DIVISIONAL AMMUNITION COLUMN

INTELLIGENCE SUMMARY

WO 40

Army Form C. 2118.

Place	Date	Hour	Summary of Events and Information	Remarks and references to Appendices
LE CATEAU	1918 Nov 3		1st Section moved to L13a.53 sheet 57B.	
	" 4		SAA Section moved to K25a68 sheet 57B. Ammunition dump formed at the FACTORY, BOUSSIES	
	" 5		Headquarters moved to LE FAYT F^{me} 1st section L5c. sheet 57B 2nd " L5a.88 " SAA " BOUSSIES	
LE FAYT F^{me}	6		2nd Section moved to A24.6.05 20. Sheet 57A	
	7		1st Section moved to SASSEGNIES (C.8central) Sheet 57A	
			SAA Section moved to LANDRECIES	
	8		2nd Section moved to C131639 Sheet 57A	
	9		Headquarters moved to H^{TE} NOYELLES	
H^{TE} NOYELLES	10		1 & 2 Section moved to REMY-CHAUSSÉE	

PAGE Nº 2

WAR DIARY 50TH DIVISIONAL AMMUNITION COLUMN
INTELLIGENCE SUMMARY
Army Form C. 2118.

(Erase heading not required.)

Place	Date	Hour	Summary of Events and Information	Remarks and references to Appendices
HTE NOYELLES	1918 Nov. 11	1100	Headquarters moved to D.13.c.56. sheet 57A (MONCEAU ST VAAST) Hostilities ceased.	
	12.		S.A.A. Section moved to HTE NOYELLES	
	16		Q.F. section moved to H.9.c.40 sheet 57A (MAROILLES)	
MONCEAU ST VAAST	19		Q.F. Section moved to J.16.c.39 sheet 57p (ST HILAIRE) S.A.A. Section moved to J.16.c.14 " "	
	to		Nos 1 & 2 Sections Billeting arrangements as " " (opposite) B.C. D.E. H.J. & K sheet 57A	
	15		A large salvage dump on D.11.19	
	19		Q.F. Section commenced salvage on J.6.9.10.11.14.15.16.17 sheet 57A	
	22		Salvaging carried on of every description	
	24		After being loaded 2 D.A.C. Wagons are sent at once to...	

PAGE No 3

Army Form C. 2118.

WAR DIARY 50TH DIVISIONAL AMMUNITION COLUMN

or

INTELLIGENCE SUMMARY.

(Erase heading not required.)

Instructions regarding War Diaries and Intelligence Summaries are contained in F. S. Regs., Part II. and the Staff Manual respectively. Title pages will be prepared in manuscript.

Place	Date	Hour	Summary of Events and Information	Remarks and references to Appendices
MONCEAU ST WAAST	1918 Nov 25		Commenced clearing of back wagons both at M1/A 2080 Sheet 57/A which consisted of all wagons on 29/11/18. These were all taken to AULNOYE.	
	30		Lections we engaged in the carrying of 18 pr and 4.5" ammunition from our 32 dump to AULNOYE.	
			Since the cessation of hostilities this unit has been very busily engaged in the salvaging of allotted areas. During the month of November an Educational Scheme was inaugurated.	

ReSBrany
Lieut Colonel RFA
Commandant 50th Divisional Ammunition Column

WAR DIARY.

OF

50TH DIVISIONAL

AMMUNITION COLUMN.

FOR

DECEMBER, 1918.

BOLUME XLV.

31.12.18.

PAGE 1.

WAR DIARY 50TH DIVISIONAL AMMUNITION COLUMN Army Form C. 2118.

or

INTELLIGENCE SUMMARY.

(Erase heading not required.)

Place	Date	Hour	Summary of Events and Information	Remarks and references to Appendices
MONCEAU ST VAAST	1918. DEC^R 1 to 17		Salvage Operations.	
	17		Headquarters, 2nd S.A.A. Section moved to FRASNOY 1st Section moved to VILLEREAU.	
	22		1st Section moved to AMFROIPRET.	
	26, 31		Engaged in salvaging of areas. Squares H.7, 8, 9, 13, 14, 15, 19, 20, 21, 25, 26, 27, 31, 32 & 33. Sheet 51	
	29		24 m.ls. belonging to SAA Sections drawn	
			During the month 214 mines & were despatched from Wild for release as coal miners.	

R. D. Zulety ? Lieut Colonel,
Commanding 50th Divl Amⁿ Column

WAR   DIARY

OF

50TH   DIVISIONAL

AMMUNITION   COLUMN

FOR

JANUARY,   1919.

VOLUME XLV/

31.1.19.

PAGE 1.

Army Form C. 2118.

WAR DIARY 50th DIVISIONAL AMMUNITION COLUMN
or
INTELLIGENCE SUMMARY.

(Erase heading not required.)

WO 95 4 2

Place	Date	Hour	Summary of Events and Information	Remarks and references to Appendices
FRASNOY	1919 Jany 1 to 31		Salvage operations. During the month 3 Officers and 61 other ranks were despatched to England for demobilization. Also 61 mules and 2 horses were despatched to TOURNAI for issue to the Belgians. RCDrury Lieut Colonel. RFA Commanding 50th Divisional Ammunition Column	

War Diary

of

50th Divisional Ammunition Column.

for
February, 1919.

Volume. XLVI

28.2.19.

RCDunny

PAGE 1

50TH DIVISIONAL AMMUNITION COLUMN

Army Form C. 2118.

WAR DIARY
or
INTELLIGENCE SUMMARY.
(Erase heading not required.)

Place	Date	Hour	Summary of Events and Information	Remarks and references to Appendices
FRANCE	1919 Jan 1 to 29		Salvage operations.	
			During the month, 4 Officers and 19 Other Ranks were despatched to England for demobilization. Also 10 horses and 15 mules were transferred to Remount Regiment and the Auxiliary for sale.	
			A draft of 150 Indians sent ashore on 1.2.19 from Indian Base Depot, Marseilles.	

Re Otway
Lieut Colonel RFA
Commanding 50th Divl Ammun Column

War Diary

— of —

50ᵀᴴ Divisional Ammunition Column.

— For —

March 1919

Volume XLVIII

31.3.19.

WAR DIARY 50TH DIVISIONAL AMMUNITION Column

Army Form C. 2118.

INTELLIGENCE SUMMARY

Vol 44

Place	Date	Hour	Summary of Events and Information	Remarks and references to Appendices
FRASNOY	1919 MARCH 1 to 31		SALVAGE OPERATIONS.	
	19th		1st Section moved to PREUX-AU-SART.	
	19th		Indian Section " "	
			During the month 1 Officers and 36 Other Ranks were despatched to England for demobilization.	
			64 Horses and 343 mules were despatched to Army of Occupation, to England, and for sale in France during the month.	

RCDrury
Lieut Colonel RFA
Commanding 50th Divl Ammn Column

War Diary

– of –

50th Divisional Ammunition Column

- for -

April 1919

Volume XLIX

1-5-19.

PAGE 1

50TH DIVISIONAL AMMUNITION COLUMN

WAR DIARY
or
INTELLIGENCE SUMMARY.
(Erase heading not required.)

Army Form C. 2118.

Vol 45

Place	Date	Hour	Summary of Events and Information	Remarks and references to Appendices
FRASNOY	1919 April 19/30		Lt. Col. R.B. Drury DSO, Captn. C.H. Jose, 2/Lieut (a/Capt) E.J. Berryman M.C. D.C.M., 2/Lieut D. Morris, 2 Sergeants, 3 Corporals, 2 Bombdrs. and 5 other ranks, and the entire Indian Section proceeded to NEUF CHATEL Pas de Calais to form a "Z" Horse Depôt under command of Lt. Col. Drury. 26 Other ranks were despatched to England for demobilisation during the month. 28 mules and 1 horse were despatched, and 8 horses received, during the month. The Column is now reduced to Cadre Strength.	

HMMeaghan, Captain R.F.A.
Commanding 50th Divl. Ammn Column

WAR DIARY

- OF -

50TH DIVISIONAL AMMUNITION COLUMN

FOR

MAY 1919.

VOLUME XLX.

1-6-1919.

Army Form C. 2118.

WAR DIARY
or
INTELLIGENCE SUMMARY.
(Erase heading not required.)

Place	Date	Hour	Summary of Events and Information	Remarks and references to Appendices
FRASNOY.	1919 May 6th		N° 1 Section moved from PREUX to FRASNOY.	
	13/14/29		26 Other Ranks were despatched to England for demobilization during the month.	
	5th/15th		6 horses were despatched & 6 horses received during the month.	

R. Wellington, Captain
50th Divisional Ammunition Column.

WAR DIARY
or
INTELLIGENCE SUMMARY.

(Erase heading not required.)

Army Form C. 2118.

50 D Am Col

Place	Date	Hour	Summary of Events and Information	Remarks and references to Appendices
FRASNOY	1919			
	28/6/19	—	The Cadre, 93 N.C.O.s & men, despatched to U.K. for demobilization.	
	1st/30th June	—	Eleven horses were despatched & ten horses received during the month.	
	30/6/19	—	One N.C.O. & eleven Other Ranks posted to R.A. Reinforcement Camp, 2nd Army (A of Occ)	

Killcullen(?) Capt, R.F.A.(T)
50th Divisional Ammunition Column.

Army Form W.3091.

Cover for Documents.

Nature of Enclosures.

WAR DIARIES,
OCTOBER. 1918.
VOL. XLIII
50th DIV. ARTY.

Notes, or Letters written.

www.ingramcontent.com/pod-product-compliance
Lightning Source LLC
Chambersburg PA
CBHW080830010526
44112CB00015B/2487